Shadows
of
Pearl

by
Arianne Richmonde

Arianne Richmonde's full-length novels in *The Pearl Trilogy*, *Shades of Pearl*, *Shadows of Pearl and Shimmers of Pearl*, follow the tumultuous and heart-rending love story between Pearl Robinson and Alexandre Chevalier. All three books are Amazon best sellers in erotic romance.

Praise for *The Pearl Trilogy:*

'*The Pearl Trilogy* is a must read!! OMG! I loved the Fifty Shades and Bared to You series…but this one is a topper!! I laughed and cried - it's so well written. So many twists and turns and just when you think you know where this story is going….you don't! It's frustrating, and oh, about every emotion you have - you'll feel it. I love the fact that it's written about a 40 year-old female…that's my age…Now, if only I could meet a hot Frenchman like Alexandre Chevalier…'

-A.J Cox.

'All three books flowed wonderfully and had the perfect ending for the wonderful trilogy. If you haven't read this trilogy yet, put it on your Must Read list!! I look forward to more from Arianne Richmonde!!'

—Sassy and Sultry Books

'The wait for this final book in the series was well worth it. There were twists I never would have imagined….the best erotica series I have read to date. Arianne Richmonde I look forward to the next book, you truly are a delight to read.'

—Megan Cain Loera

Praise for *Shades of Pearl:*

'This was a great book, Pearl was such a great character that she won me over from the start. The sex scenes were just how I like them, hot heavy and very sensual when the time was right, I loved the fairytale aspect to this book, the great hero, the female lead who had traits she did not like about herself, the evil family member, I would highly recommend this to all who love a great love story with sex, that would be most of us then, 5/5'

—*Confessions of a Bookaholic*

'I recommend this book for those who enjoy a wonderfully written first person narrative, romantic erotica, with lots of dialogue and plenty of well-done descriptive scenes.'

—*Swept Away By Romance*

'*Shades of Pearl* has been written to an exceptional standard, it captivates its audience from the first page and keeps you entertained until the very end. The characters are so well described, allowing images to run wild in your head. The story makes you laugh, scream and cry and leaves you wanting more.'

—*Nade Ferrabee*

'As a fan of the erotica genre and, most recently, the 50 Shades phenomenon, I was thrilled to find this book so incredibly steamy but without the hard side of hard kink to it.'

—*Jenny Baldwin*

Praise for *Shadows of Pearl:*

'I'm mad, I'm sad, I've been crying, I want to hit some characters in the book…well more than one person actually!

This book was an **AMAZING** read for me. It started off where *Shades of Pearl* left off. The book grabbed me right from the start and I did not want to put it down. I personally love Arianne Richmonde's writing style. I think she did an excellent job with these characters and the story line was VERY original.

I WANT BOOK 3 NOW!! I need to know what will happen next. Arianne left this reader wanting and needing **MORE**. I know without a doubt, that book 3 is a **MUST READ** for me!'

—*Swept Away By Romance*

'Let me say that ***Shadows of Pearl*** made for a FREAKING awesome story filled with so much drama…oh, how I loved the drama. It was a big page turner for me and when things got crazy oh how I got sucked in!'

—*Momma's Books Blog*

'I am a fan of the 50 Shades of Grey series and the Bared to You series. As I liked both this one was a surprise and I loved it. I thought this was better than both of them put together. I found a new author who can't write fast enough. Arianne Richmonde is a new fave for me.'

—*Amazon reviewer*

'This book has twists and turns that I never expected. I thought this might be another knock off of Fifty but Oh, no! This book holds it's own and I loved every word of it!'

—*Samantha Addison*

Praise for *Shimmers of Pearl:*

'Awesome; full of heart, tears and much laughter. This book flows together and feels so real and true I forgot I was actually reading a story. I love these characters. If you want to read something great, get these books.'

—Dawn M. Earley

'Wow, this had me on the edge of my seat, or rather bed. I have loved the whole trilogy of Pearl & I am sad that this is the end, I love how this author writes, she made me believe I was watching the whole thing like a film in my head which is just how I like to read my books, watching them play out and imagining the characters.'

—Confessions of a Bookaholic

'*Shimmers of Pearl* is what a true erotic book should be; great story line, wonderful characters, and some of the **HOTTEST** sex/love scenes I've read in a while. This is where the author's writing shines. I could really feel the attraction and desire that Pearl and Alexandre had for each other. Their chemistry was amazing and their need for each other leapt off the pages.
Arianne Richmonde did a wonderful job, not with just the story and characters but also with her skillfully crafted descriptive writing. The whole Pearl Trilogy has simply captivated me.'

—Swept Away by Romance

'Holy hotness for sure! Arianne Richmonde more than delivered with book 3!!!'

—Sassy and Sultry Books

About the Author

Arianne Richmonde is an American writer and artist who was raised in both the US and Europe. She lives in France with her husband.

As well as *The Pearl Trilogy* novels she has written a short story, *Glass*. She is currently writing her next novel, *Pearl*, from Alexandre's point of view.

For more information on the author visit her website:

www.ariannerichmonde.com

Dedication

To all my wonderful readers who demanded more. Thanks for all your love, support and feedback. This would never have happened without you.

Acknowledgements

To my husband for his amazing help with everything technical (ssh…he still hasn't read a word and hopefully never will).

Brooke for being my first reader for *Shades of Pearl*, thinking it was all a hoot, that I was very naughty - nevertheless championing me all the way. Angela for being a true friend even though we've never met. Sam, Nade and so many fabulous readers (you know who you are) who have given me feedback, recommended my book to others and been more than supportive. Lisa and Cheryl for their eagle eyes. Paul at BB eBooks for his skill, patience and looking after me so well.

And last but not least, the fabulous and talented Zang Toi, master of creation and a true friend.

1

I'm lying between the glorious Egyptian cotton sheets in Alexandre's bed, relaxing against the plumped-up, down feather pillows. I feel satiated. Complete, both physically and spiritually. Beyond satisfied. More glorious love-making has left me feeling like the luckiest, most appreciated woman in the world.

Of all people, I know what it's like to be stuck in a sexual desert – without another human being to fulfill my needs. For almost twenty years I had convinced myself that work could be a substitute. I'd given up. I'd learned to be self-sufficient in every way – yes, in *every* way - and I never, in a million years, believed that at forty years old I would meet anyone special, let alone a man fifteen years my junior. And not only a man younger than I was; but ridiculously successful, kind, devastatingly handsome and last but not least, a veritable god in bed.

And to top it all off; completely in love with me...

Alexandre Chevalier.

I still feel as if I have walked into a modern day fairy tale.

It's tough when you're riddled with insecurities the way I am. Hard to believe that a man so gorgeous can covet you and feel the same intensity of passion that you feel for him. Yet, there he was, Alexandre Chevalier, co-founder of the Internet sensation HookedUp – a company which has taken the world by storm and, at the tender age of twenty-five, has made him into one of the wealthiest men in the world. There Alexandre was - wanting to date me.

And if that wasn't enough, he has chosen me, Pearl Robinson, a forty year-old with my just-above-average, girl-next-door looks, to be his *wife*.

Yes, I do believe I'm dreaming.

I look now at my left hand which I'm turning this way and that and admire my diamond engagement ring - proof that all this is real. It's glinting, catching rays of morning sunlight which are pouring in through the long bedroom window. The ice-blue silk drapes are half open. Alexandre hates to sleep with them closed - as if darkness could swallow him up at dawn.

I've learned a lot about Alexandre in the two months since we've been engaged. There's a shadow that lives within - a mood which can encompass him at times, and it frightens me. I can never be sure when it will possess him but it is there, deep inside his soul. He's a damaged man - that much I know. Yet he seems to be an expert at hiding the phantoms which lurk within.

So far, I have only seen glimpses.

I too, try to hide any gremlins from my past. Some things are better left unsaid. We are still getting to know each other.

I can hear him now, next door in the en-suite bathroom. The

faucet has just been turned off. I picture him in my mind's eye; water trickling from his lightly tanned chest, his biceps flexed deliciously as he dries himself, his strong, muscular thighs, the ripples of his stomach and his wet, almost-black hair - wayward and mussed-up - which frames the even features of his handsome face.

I think of our lovemaking just ten minutes ago and a shiver of lust shimmies through my body. I cannot get enough of him. He possesses my psyche. I have never needed anybody as I need him. But I try to keep myself cool, calm and collected, even though I'm on fire inside. He mustn't know the apprehension that envelops me - fear that I could be flung back again into the desert, abandoned with no water - on my own once more. And when I say 'on my own' I don't mean literally so. No, you can be with a man and feel like an island – as I was with my ex-husband, Saul. I blamed myself for my frigidity, my inability to reach orgasm through sex which, if I remember correctly, happened in my early twenties after I'd split up with my first boyfriend, Brad.

I thought I was a lost cause until I met Alexandre. He intrinsically understands me and my body. Maybe that's why I'm hooked on him. Sexually. Mentally. But I try to keep that to myself. There's nothing like a needy woman to scare a man away. Especially one as hot as he is. I have to hold onto my independence, my self-possession.

Or I could lose him for good.

My fiancé saunters into the bedroom and fixes his eyes on me, running them along my naked body with approval. I cannot believe he is actually mine. *My fiancé.* How I relish those words.

I'm now willing him with my gaze to come back to bed, just for ten minutes, but I know that his drive and ambition rarely lets him lose restraint. He has a plane to catch – a business trip is waiting; clients hanging in limbo with baited breath for a decision to be made, a deal to be signed. I've learned that Alexandre is a ruthless negotiator, a tough cookie when it comes to business – nobody gets to be as successful as he is by accident.

I drink him in. A white towel is hanging about his washboard abs. Beads of water are gathered about his buffed-up chest. His green eyes are gazing at me.

"Come with me, Pearl," he says, his French accent full and rich.

"I told you, I really can't."

"I'd love to show you my favorite haunts in London, take you to the theatre, a walk along the South Bank by the River Thames."

He moves over to the bed and sits beside me, fondling my chin with his long fingers. He tilts my head back a touch and presses his lips to mine. His tongue explores my mouth, the tip of it gently probing, running along my lips. He holds my head in his hands and teases my tongue with his. I feel the electricity of it - tingles shoot between my thighs. I groan. My sound makes his kiss more intense, hungrier. The towel moves - his huge cock is flexing against it. I rest my hand there and feel how stiff it is. Always ready for me, even with just a kiss or at the sight of my naked body. Nobody has ever desired me the way he does.

"Why are you tormenting me like this?" he whispers. "You know I don't like us being apart."

"I can't just leave Anthony alone – he's come all the way from San Francisco to visit. Besides, I told you, I have that important meeting this morning."

"It's just work, it can be postponed."

"No, it can't. Samuel Myers has flown in from LA. You can't start up a company for me, Alexandre, and then expect it to run itself. HookedUp Enterprises needs me more than ever right now – it's my baby."

"So têtue," he teases, his French accent rumblingly deep.

"What does that mean?"

"Stubborn."

I laugh. "I know you, Alexandre Chevalier. You told me once yourself, that the last thing you wanted was a woman to be hanging onto your 'every word, your every movement' – that's what you said. You'd get bored of me if I didn't have my own projects, my own life."

"Perhaps, but sometimes I think you push it, Pearl. Like the wedding, for instance. Why are you making us wait until December? It's absurd – we could get married as soon as I get back from London." He grazes his tongue along my lips and kisses me again.

"I told you - I've always dreamed of a winter wedding," I whisper.

"The ice princess."

I trace my fingers along his cheekbone and smile. Let him think I'm the ice princess. Let him think I'm cool. He can't know that my insides are made of marshmallow – that my need for him is more than life itself.

"You'll be late," I warn, running my fingers through his thick, soft hair.

"What I like though, is when I fuck you I make you melt," he murmurs, his hands trailing down my back along my spine. "I love your dimples, these adorable dimples in your back, just here…and here." He makes circular motions around my little dips and then runs the tips of his fingers further south, cupping my buttocks in his large hands.

I feel the tips of his fingers as they lightly, so very lightly touch my moist folds, lifting me off the mattress, pulling me towards him. "So wet," he says. "Even when all I do is kiss you. Funny how you and I get each other so worked up - you've made me rock hard."

"Yes…isn't it?" We both laugh.

"Shit, damn it! You're so tempting, Pearl. Damn my meeting." He nips my lower lip softly between his minty teeth.

The tease - I'm used to this. He keeps me in check – always leaving me begging for more, my heart racing. Pick any V name you like – vagina, Vajajay or my pet names, V-8 and Venus. That part of me throbs with desire, aching for his return – even before he has departed. Or even when he's right beside me, my Venus is on red alert, ready to go at a moment's notice. Alexandre says he likes it this way. My resolve must stay intact, though. I need to stay strong. I cannot lose myself in him one hundred percent.

Or he'd swallow me whole.

I study him. It's not just sex that has me in his hold. It's the way he is inside; his kindness, generosity, his sense of humor, the love he has for me - even his damn French pride which makes him a touch possessive and jealous. Not too much - no, but just enough to make me feel desired and treasured. All this makes up a complex personality - a character I'm still trying to work out.

He walks over to his closet and opens the door. That same closet where, just three months ago, I hid myself behind rows of hand-tailored suits and racks of silk ties – where I childishly played Hide and Seek. A tremor fills my body now, remembering that sexually-charged moment. Alexandre caught me and then tied my legs to the bedposts with two ice-blue silk ties, splaying my thighs apart. I thought he was going to play bondage and he did. His style. Sweet - but terrifying as I couldn't imagine what would happen next. I had nothing to fear; he 'beat' me with a Kingfisher feather and tied my wrists together behind my head with the priceless Art Deco pearl choker he bought me in Paris. The excitement tipped me over the edge – the trepidation, the lust, the sensitivity all mixed together in a delicious cocktail of sex. A cocktail which has turned me into an alcoholic of love. A drink which I need every day just to function at my best.

I am addicted to him.

I watch him now. Six feet, three inches of pure, virile male. What is it that makes me want him to take charge in the bedroom? To overpower me? I love being beneath him, strong and dominant as he is – on top of me, pushing me to my limits, making me scream his name when I come. He has control over me sexually and he knows it – I can't let him also dominate my life. He's testing me. I can sense it. Testing me to see how strong I can be. He made it clear that he wants an equal. I have to match him; I cannot let myself sink into oblivion. He once told me he was attracted to me for my maturity and that he was into 'women not girls' – I need to act my age – keep my composure. It's a battle I fight every day. I still feel like a vulnerable child inside and sometimes find myself acting like a teenager with her first love. Passion is a powerful thing – hard to control.

"What's it to be today - T-shirt and jeans, or a suit?" I ask him.

He pulls on a pair of boxer briefs over his tight, perfectly formed butt. My eyes then focus on that fine smooth hairline that goes from his abs down to his groin. He still has a semi-erection bulking out his underwear. He looks at me. "I don't know, what do you think?"

"Both are sexy. The second you put a suit on I want you to fuck me, though - you fully-clothed with just your cock free. You could take me up against the wall. I love it when I'm naked and you're dressed in one of your chic, tailored suits. I love it when you slam me from behind." I bite my lip. "Hard as a rock. Just thinking about it makes me so−"

"Stop tormenting me, baby, or I'll have to put you over my knee and spank you." He winks at me.

"That'll be the day."

"You know I could never do that, Pearl, not even in jest."

I observe him as he pulls out a pair of jeans and a black T-shirt from the rack in the closet. "Jeans it is, then," he says assertively, "or I'll never get to London on time."

"Bastard," I say with a grin.

"It's not as if I haven't asked you to come with me. It's not too late to change your mind."

"No, I'm staying."

"Sure? Last call−"

"I'm sure," I say, already regretful.

I slip out of the bed and glide towards him. "I'll miss you." I place my arms about his warm, strong torso and hold myself close to him. I breathe in his faint smell of lavender, hand-picked from his fields in Provence - crushed into heavenly oil - and the famous wish-I-could-bottle Alexandre smell - his natural odor that has me completely intoxicated.

As if on cue, Rex bounds his way into the bedroom, excited from his morning walk. He often barges in on our intimate moments. His black Labrador-mix tail spins about like a windmill; his tight muscles rival his master's.

"Oh Rex, how I'll miss you my boy," Alexandre says, bending down to hug his dog. "Look after him for me, Pearl. Don't let Anthony spoil him with too many treats. I'm late, I have to rush. See you in a couple of days." He embraces us in a family trio and then looks into my eyes and says, "I love you, Pearl. You're my everything - my light, my future. Take care now." He plants another kiss on my lips and makes his way down the corridor to the elevator where his ready-packed case is waiting. I don't follow as I'm still naked. Anthony is staying in one of the guest rooms – God forbid my brother should see me with no clothes on.

Anthony is in his element. He arrived late last night and couldn't believe that Alexandre's chauffeur was there to meet him at the airport. He tells me that he's moving in (joke). Or is it? Anthony could get used to this lifestyle. Not to mention his boy-crush on Alexandre.

I get dressed and find breakfast waiting in the kitchen. Coffee, cereals, home-made yoghurt and jellies, fresh fruit and a spread of croissants and pastries sit temptingly on the table. I begin to set things on a tray to send up to the roof terrace. Sun is streaming through the windows and the sky is crystal blue. The perfect Fall weather. Cool, sunny and crisp but warm enough to still eat outside. Patricia, one of the staff, finds me rummaging about the kitchen and a look of dismay shadows her face. She's wearing a neat, black and white uniform – her choice – she says she feels more professional that way.

"Ms. Pearl, please, what are you doing? You'll make me lose my job if you insist on serving yourself."

"I doubt that, Patricia. I thought Anthony and I could sit on the rooftop, have breakfast up there, today, but I don't want to be a nuisance."

"That's what the Dumbwaiter's for," she says with a wink.

"Best invention ever," I agree.

She loads everything into the mini-elevator which sends food or forgotten cell phones up and down between floors. Anthony has not yet set eyes on this marvel. I can hear him now in the living room screaming and yelping.

"Thanks, Patricia. I'm going to take my excitable brother upstairs."

I find Anthony sitting on the piano stool, breathless, his mouth open so far that his jaw is practically horizontal to the floor. He catches my eye as I'm standing in the doorway.

"Oh my GOD!"

"I know," I reply simply.

"Pearleee—"

"Do you want me to call 911?"

"Oh my freakin' God!"

"Yes, I think God has got the point."

"What is this place? A *museum*? I mean, this room is the size of mine and Bruce's entire apartment in San Francisco!"

"It is pretty awesome."

"Awesome does not even begin to describe this *palace*."

I watch his eyes scan the room; the walnut wood paneled walls, the delicate cabinetry and integrated bookshelves, the parquet floor, the picture windows with views of Central Park on one side and of The Plaza on the other - and the massive marble fireplaces. Rex is wagging his tail as if in agreement. He came from humble beginnings - from a dog pound in Paris – where the poor thing was waiting on Death Row. I get the feeling that he, too, appreciates his luxurious surroundings. Anthony is now caressing the piano keys; whimpering sounds are emanating from somewhere deep within his body as if he were sick with fever.

"Can you imagine having a grand piano like this?" he gushes.

"I don't have to imagine it, Anthony – it's a reality."

"Have you pinched yourself? Are you sure you're not just dreaming?"

"Sometimes I do wonder."

"A Steinway? Seriously? I really do have heart palpitations - you need to call an ambulance."

"Play something, Ant."

"Are you talkin' to me? Are you talking to *me*?" he jokes, imitating Robert de Niro in *Taxi Driver*. "Are you talking to *me*? Well, I'm the only one here!"

I burst out laughing. Anthony couldn't look more unlike Travis Bickle if he tried. My brother is heavy, blonde – okay, not heavy - he is actively overweight. And when I say actively, I mean he cannot stop eating, even though every day he swears he has started a new diet. I've missed him – he does make me laugh. Except when I'm the object of his humor, which is often.

He begins to play and within seconds my eyes well with tears from the beauty of the sound. The way he strokes the keys with such a whispery touch makes me remember what a novice I am compared to him in the musical department. He has so much talent I find myself holding my breath.

"Mom used to sing this to us to get us to fall asleep. Do you remember?" He's playing *Lullaby* by Brahms.

"I miss her so much," I tell him quietly.

But he doesn't reply. His answer is all in his playing. His fingers caress the keys and his eyes, half closed, speak of nostalgia for a life cut short; a woman we both loved beyond measure who was taken from us too soon – her bones ravaged by that evil disease which begins with C and ends in heartbreak. Before I know it, I'm weeping, as if all my pain has finally unleashed itself. Pearl, the Independent One can finally let loose her pent-up sorrow.

"Why her?" I mumble. "Why her…"

Anthony stops his playing short. "I know. I know."

I take his hand and try to change the mood, "Breakfast, come on! You think this room is cool? You ain't seen nuthin' yet," I joke, "wait till you see the roof terrace."

I lead him upstairs, Rex excitedly at our heels, and listen to Anthony's oohs and ahs as he flips out about the décor, the priceless antique furniture and works of art. His eyes settle on a giant, red, heart painting with a multi-colored background. "That's a Jim Dine," he observes, "isn't it? A. Goddam. Jim. Freakin. Goddam. Dine!"

"Alexandre gave that to me a few weeks ago. An engagement present."

"Oh, so like, the rock of a diamond solitaire you're wearing on your finger wasn't enough already?"

I laugh. "Obscene, isn't it?"

"Well, it is *big*, to say the least."

"It belonged to a Russian princess."

He raises an eyebrow. "Of course it did."

"The diamond was part of a pendant and Alexandre had it made into a ring."

Anthony's reaction to the roof terrace with its real lawn, trees and sumptuous views across Central Park and the Manhattan skyline is even more extreme than mine was the first time I laid eyes on it all, back in June. "So the view wasn't enough… there has to be a freakin' *park* on top of this roof *as well?*"

"All for Rex," I say.

"I'm going to dress up as a dog."

I pull my cardigan tighter about my waist. "It's a little cool, let's go into the orangery and have breakfast."

"Don't we need to take Rex for a walk in the park first? Do his poops and stuff?"

"Don't worry, he's been out already."

"You took him out this morning so early?"

"No, Rex has a kind of nanny. She comes every morning at 7am sharp. Then again at eleven and every four hours if somebody's home. If I'm at work then his nanny – her name's Sally - she hangs out with him. Rex is never alone."

"You're kidding me."

I giggle. "No, really. Rex lives up to his name. He's a king."

"I'll say."

"Come here, Rex, let me see that new collar you're wearing." He wiggles up to me sporting a smart, electric blue collar. He's wagging proudly. "Sally must have bought him that; she's always getting him gifts."

"So who else is running the show, besides Rex's nanny?"

"The housekeeper, Patricia, two or three cleaning ladies, a chef who comes and goes if Alexandre isn't in the mood to cook and−"

Anthony interrupts me with a waving hand. "Stop! I've heard enough, I can feel myself turning green."

I pour some coffee for us both and he's staring at me as if dissecting my very being. Uh, oh, what now…

"Pearl, what is wrong with you?"

"Excuse me?"

"What the hell are you playing at with this winter wedding bullshit. Winter - hello - is two months away. What are you waiting for?"

"Look, Alexandre and I have only known each other for just over four months. I want to be absolutely sure."

"Sure of what? That you're even luckier than Kate Middleton?"

"I don't want to make a mistake. I want for us to really know each other, warts and all."

"You want him to know about your *warts?* Are you crazy? Snap him up now before he realizes what's happened. You don't want him to see your goddam warts or he could change his mind!"

"Thanks for the vote of confidence, Ant. Actually, that expression is kind of gross. Let's just say I want us to be great friends as well as lovers before we tie the knot. I want to be open about everything and anything concerning my past and for him to do the same with me."

"Are you *insane?* Keep your goddam mouth *shut* about anything at all that makes you seem less than perfect. Keep any skeletons you may have locked firmly in the closet. You cannot jeopardize this golden opportunity."

"I want us to be honest with each other."

Anthony doesn't hear me – he rattles on, "Okay, I get the whole fairytale wedding thing in Lapland. I do. The whole reindeer pulling the sled, the white, silk-velvet ribbons on their antlers, the powdery snow – I get it, but please, don't be a fool – you need to get on with this marriage already and stop dithering about."

"You want me to settle for a quick wedding just in case my

fiancé changes his mind? If he changes his mind, then I would have done the right thing. If he's that mercurial I shouldn't have been thinking about being with him in the first place."

Anthony rolls his eyes. "What's the worst that can happen? The marriage fails and you end up with a nice settlement, thank you very much."

"No, Anthony, that is *not* the plan. I would never marry for money, you know that. I refused to take a dime from Saul. In fact, I ended up lending him a ton of money which he never paid back and I never even asked him for it. I've suggested to Alexandre that we do a pre-nup. That way, it's clear from the outset that I don't want a cent if it turns out we aren't made for each other."

Anthony buries his head in his hands. His exasperation is palpable. "Please, Pearl, stop. I just can't *bear* hearing you throw your life away."

"I'm being practical. Realistic. Strong."

"You're being a dumbass – burning all your bridges. What does Alexandre say about this pre-nup nonsense?"

"He says no, and that he doesn't even want to discuss it."

"Phew, that's lucky."

"Try one of these Danish pastries – they melt in your mouth," I say, offering him a platter of tempting goodies, knowing that's the only thing that will shut Anthony up - at least for a while.

But all he does is stuff the pastry in his gob and talk with his mouth full. "And what's with all this business you've started together, this HookedUp thingamyjig?"

"HookedUp Enterprises."

"Yeah. Why can't you be content with just being a trophy

wife, so to speak? You'd never have to work again in your life."

"That is *so* not my style and you know it. Besides, Alexandre secretly likes me being into my career. He bought up Haslit Films. It's all under the umbrella of his new company, HookedUp Enterprises, run by me. And he and I are the directors of it, except he's a silent partner. He doesn't want any say in how the company's run day to day – it's all up to me. So he *says*, but I'll need his help. I want him there – I'm not that proficient with the business side of things. We've started doing feature films, keeping on Haslit for the documentary side."

"So where does that leave your boss, Natalie?"

"She's on board, too. She came with the package."

"So wait, that means you are now technically Natalie's boss and the tables have turned and you're like, some big shot who's going to hang out with Tom Cruise and Matt Bomer and all those sexy TV and movie sirens?"

I laugh and breathe in the heady scent of winter jasmine entwined about the trellises of the orangery. "Who knows where it could lead – it's exciting though."

Anthony taps his finger on his nose. "Just exactly how rich is your husband to-be? That is, if you move your skinny ass and hurry up and marry him and don't blow it all, somehow."

"Alexandre is a very powerful man. Much more powerful than I had first imagined."

"Not to mention drop-dead gorgeous. If he wasn't going to be my future brother-in-law, I swear I'd−"

"Anthony, please – you'll shock Rex."

"Sorry - go on, you were saying…"

"I actually had no idea how wealthy he was – his T-shirt and jeans look kinda had me fooled."

"Doesn't he wear a suit to meet clients?"

"Very rarely. Only if the clients are way older."

Anthony narrows his blue eyes. "Isn't everyone way older? I mean, he's only twenty-five, right?"

"He's very laid back about the way he presents himself. On the outside, that is. But I've overheard him speak business on the phone. I wouldn't want to cross him, that's for sure. Although he never raises his voice and he's always polite and friendly, but there's a kind of chilling power he holds over people. I can't explain it."

Anthony is still devouring his Danish. "A computer coder, huh?"

I take a sip of coffee. "That was what he led me to believe when I first met him. He's very modest - it's his French upbringing. He never discusses money or boasts about his wealth. He likes to make out he's just a regular guy."

"And what about Psycho-sister – does she get a stake in this new company of yours?"

"Sophie? No, this has nothing to do with her." I look at my watch. "Oh my God, Anthony, speaking of my new company – I need to run or I'll be late for my meeting. Will you be okay on your own?"

"Hell yeah, are you kidding? I get to play king of the castle."

"Sorry, that's Rex's role, isn't it sweetheart?" I say cupping Rex's wide black head in my hands and giving him a kiss on the snout.

"Ha, ha, Rex means king in Latin – very cute."

"Be good, big brother and don't get into mischief. If you need anything Patricia can help. See you later."

"Later, baby sis."

2

This is my first official meeting with a new client at HookedUp Enterprises. We have spoken several times on the phone already and even signed a preliminary deal but this is the first time we are to meet face to face.

I'm obviously nervous but I feel poised in my sharp, navy blue suit and high heels. I'm meeting a big Hollywood mogul named Samuel Myers – the old-school type who smokes a cigar and calls women 'sweetheart'. But he's friendly and easy going. A little too much for my liking.

As I approach him he looks me up and down but then his eyes wander to my engagement ring and he clears his throat as if to say, 'okay, never mind'. I smile at him. I'm used to these types - one of my first jobs was a stint in LA as a casting director's assistant. This man doesn't faze me at all.

He has been waiting for me in our lobby, a cool, modern space with vast opaque glass doors that smoothly open as you approach them. We shake hands and introduce ourselves and I lead him into my office. The windows here look down onto Fifty Seventh Street. There's a large glass desk and sleek sofas and chairs all in off-white or cool-gray leather. It is the antithesis of Alexandre's apartment. Here we are talking state-of-the-art, Italian - very contemporary.

Just as Samuel Myers has eased himself into one of the brand new designer couches and I have sat myself down and crossed my legs neatly on my swivel chair, my cell buzzes. I look down and see a message has come in from Alexandre. I know I shouldn't but I can't resist. I quickly read it.

Just remembering you naked on the bed this morning has made me hard. Can't stop thinking about your tits and ass and making you come. Can't wait to get home and fuck you senseless. X

Bastard – he knew exactly what time this meeting was. He has ways of keeping me in check. Or is it another test? To see if I'll break? See if I'll be able to remain composed. A second ago I was cool and poised. Now I feel a rush of adrenaline and heat surge through my body. I squeeze my legs together. Uh oh, no, I mustn't do that or you-know-*what* could happen. My heart's racing from Alexandre's schoolboy message, my breath short. Who would think that a forty year-old could be knocked out like this every time the one she loves comes on to her? But 40 is just a number. When you're in your twenties it seems like light years away. You imagine a forty year-old to have all the answers, never to lose her self-possession – basically, to be a grown-up. But it's not like that when you're in love. Especially when it catches you off guard the way it did for me. When you feel the way I do about someone all your barriers come crashing down. I was a woman when I met Alexandre and he changed me into a teenager.

Get a grip, Pearl.

I switch off my cell so I can't be distracted again and continue with my conversation with this important producer. I take a deep breath and say, "I read the script changes." Samuel Myers is now lounging comfortably – his weighty body spread out like a sea lion. "I think they're great," I add.

"I'm so pleased," he replies with a grin.

I sit erect and try to turn my imagination into a blank canvas – erase the image of Alexandre and his erection. "I know we signed on this project already but have you considered the leads going to women?" I ask calmly.

The producer's eyebrows shoot up. "W*omen?*"

"Yes, women."

"But, sweetheart, this is a *buddy* movie."

"Flipping gender roles works in a buddy movie. Think about *Thelma and Louise*. It beyond worked - it's a classic. You get my point."

He temples his fat, sausage-like fingers. "I hadn't even considered that."

"Would you like to think about it? Sleep on it?"

He gets up and pads his heavy frame over to the high window and looks down onto the street below. The usual background of New York City can be heard – muted by the thick triple-glazed windows, but still evident - the sirens never sleep, not in Manhattan. People below are rushing this way and that like ants on a mission. Samuel Myers snorts. "What are you saying? That if

I don't consider the leads going to actresses you'll be unhappy?"

"Let's just say that HookedUp Enterprises will be less enthusiastic about doing future projects with you unless we feel we can make our mark. We want to put our stamp on the movie industry – shake things up a bit, not just churn out the usual run-of-the-mill, same-old-same-old blockbuster. We'd like to see more females in lead roles and less ageism when it comes to actresses. There is no reason why beautiful leading women always have to be in their twenties. That message is getting worn and tired, and frankly, you're losing a big chunk of the audience that way."

"Oh."

I edge towards this powerful man and say, "There are some amazing, very sexy actresses in their late thirties, early forties: Charlize Theron, Jennifer Aniston, Cameron Diaz, Cate Blanchett, Gwyneth Paltrow, Nicole Kidman, Catherine Zeta-Jones, Lucy Liu–"

"Lucy Liu is Asian."

"So? She'd be right for the part of Sunny. She's beautiful as well as feisty."

"I don't know, I can't afford two names, Pearl."

I keep talking. "Those are just the big stars. There's a lot of other talent out there, too."

I can hear his heavy, considered breathing.

"There's nothing in that script that dictates to us that a man should play those roles," I go on, "a woman can kick ass just as easily, excuse the expression. I see *women* playing those parts."

"Okay, Pearl, let me think this through. I need to make some calls. This has taken me by surprise. Quite a ball-buster, aren't you?"

"No, Mr. Myers, I'm a pussycat."

He looks at my ring and then says, "Does your fiancé know what he's letting himself in for?"

"No, he doesn't. I thought I'd surprise him."

He chuckles. "Call me Sam, by the way."

I shake hands with him to denote the end of the meeting. I mean, there really isn't much more to discuss –either he goes for my pitch or he doesn't. "Okay, Sam, let's take a rain check. Call me as soon as you've thought this over."

"So you're not flexible on this woman thing?" he asks.

"I'm always flexible but the 'woman thing,' as you describe it, is an important factor, like it or not. We females do make up almost half of the world's population and we're pretty bored of playing second fiddle all the time."

"A feminist."

"Not a feminist, just a woman. But you can't be a woman in today's world without busting the odd ball here or there." I give him a wry smile and he laughs. "We'll speak later," I say assertively. "Call me."

I walk him to the elevator and when he's out of sight I punch my fists in the air. "Yes!" I never imagined he'd even *consider* letting the roles go to women. I call Alexandre to tell him the good news. No answer. He must be in the air. As I pass back by the lobby, Jeanine, our receptionist, an ice-cool brunette who matches the décor perfectly she's so glamorous, tells me in a husky voice. "Pearl, there's a video clip waiting for you."

Alexandre and I have instructed everyone who works here to call us by our first names. No pretentions here. We want to make everyone at HookedUp Enterprises feel like extended family.

"Samuel Myers brought in a video? He forgot to mention

22

that."

"No, your fiancé," she says emphasizing the F of fiancé.

"Alexandre? When?"

He called me ten minutes ago. You weren't picking up, he said. Check your email. There should be a video in your messages."

"Thank you, Jeanine."

"You're welcome."

I go back into my office and look through my emails. There is an attachment. I click on it. I simultaneously laugh and cover my mouth with my hand in shock. I should be used to this by now but Alexandre's shenanigans still take me by surprise. He's lying on a bed in the private jet. Then the focus zooms in on his huge penis taking up the whole screen. He must have shot this with his iPhone. There it is - smooth as silk in its full glory, hard and thick as granite, the head proud. His hand grips it as he lies on the bed propped up against cushions – the self-held camera pans up - he's languidly seductive, his eyes half closed, his tongue running lustfully along his dark red lips. I hear his deep voice. "Chérie, I'm on the plane before take-off in this private cabin thinking of you, kicking myself that I didn't force you to come with me today. I miss you already."

I'm hot and feel a throb between my legs. The sight of Alexandre's huge penis has my heart beating fast, my whole body tingling. I press my fingers on my clit and give it a hard push. Oh yeah. I look at the screen and am transfixed as he fondles himself and starts moving his gripped hand tightly around his erection. He goes on, "I'm thinking of your wet pearlette, Pearl, and your beautiful face when you come for me and your erect nipples and that pretty waist and soft skin and I'm thinking how when I get home I'm going to tease you with my cock. I'm going to bend you over the arm of the sofa and flutter my tongue around your clit. Just the tip of my tongue. Really gently. I know you baby, you're gonna get all wet and hot and be begging me for it. And I'll make you wait. I'll make you moan with anticipation."

I swallow. I can feel my pulse speed up hearing his words, imagining myself in the position he describes. I press 'pause' and go over to my office door and lock it. Jeanine always knocks, but just to be sure. I go back to my laptop and press 'play' again.

"See how hard I am?" he purrs. "I'm thinking of you sucking me – your pretty lips wrapped around my cock, running your tongue up and down and making it even stiffer."

I unzip my skirt and let it pool around my ankles on the floor. I take off my suit jacket and fling it on the back of my swivel chair.

Alexandre continues. "Have you got your fingers in your pussy, baby? Is it all wet for me? I want you to sit back in your chair with your legs wide open…"

Wait a minute, I think, how does he know I'm next to my chair? I sit down, my heart pounding, and yes, I am wet. Very wet.

"Let's get back to the other position I had in mind for you, eh?" he says, the focus now on his face which is grimacing from pleasuring himself. "You bent over the sofa arm, your peachy ass in the air. I'm gonna have to spank that ass, baby and then I'm going to take you from behind."

He has never spanked me, ever, but he talks about it in his fantasies – does he do that to please me, or does he secretly want to punish me? I still don't know.

"I'll slip my cock in just an inch, no more. Thrust it in all the way, and then out, and then tease you again with just a centimeter of my cock. You won't know when I'm going to slam you. Maybe I'll pump you good and hard, maybe I won't. Maybe you'll be screaming for me to fuck you."

My fingers are deep inside myself now. I'm hooking them up against my front wall against my G-spot - a place I didn't even know existed until Alexandre found it with his magic thumb. My left hand is on top, both adding pressure now to my clit and my special zone. I make circular movements and press harder now. I can feel the build-up. My eyes are glued to the screen. The camera is back on his rock-hard cock and he's moaning now, almost growling – he's about to come – I can sense it.

"All I can think about is fucking you. I. Love. Fucking. You. Pearl. I love fucking you hard, fucking, you, really slow."

I suddenly hear a knock as I'm about to reach orgasm. The panic of it makes me climax in a thunderous spasm. But then I realize the knock's coming from Alexandre's home-made porn movie as I hear him shout out, "hang on, just coming."

"We're about to take off, sir, I need you to buckle-up," a muffled voice says through the cabin door.

He groans. I watch his face, now shown up by the camera in twisted ecstasy, and I laugh at the madness and irony of it all – 'just coming' he said - and I'm still coming, too, with delicious, powerful contractions – never were words more aptly spoken.

Then the video goes dead.

Why does Alexandre continually make me feel like a naughty schoolgirl?

I try to compose myself, which is difficult as now all I have on the brain is my sexy fiancé. I'm not the jealous type but I wonder at my foolishness of letting him roam free in London without me there by his side. I trust him, I do, but at the end of the day he's still a guy. Women throw themselves at him. Women, girls, mothers, dogs; this is a man who enjoys popularity. He's easygoing and nearly always has a gentle smile on his lips which makes him very attractive to everyone. But there's also something commandeering about him that make people sit up and pay attention.

Funny, he says the same about me – that people listen. I do a good job of pretending – shoulders back, head up (and all that) but inside I feel the same as when I was twelve years old. You think getting older would make you qualify in the extra confidence stakes, but it doesn't. Perhaps all that happens is that you get better at acting. If I have him fooled, that's fine by me. If I have Samuel Myers fooled – all the better.

I go to the bathroom to freshen up. One thing Alexandre has had installed in every bathroom in his apartment and here is the old-fashioned bidet. At first, I thought it was archaic but now I'm a convert and wince every time I go to a bathroom and there isn't one. How civilized they are – perfect for a quick clean-up at any moment, especially if you've indulged in a little afternoon sex and don't have time for a shower. I have found they are perfect to use as a foot-bath, too.

I look in the mirror and see a happy woman staring back at me. Her skin is glowing, her blue-gray eyes bright. Lots of passionate sex – the perfect cure for anyone.

I turn my cell back on and see I have three messages. Alexandre? No, Anthony. My mind flashes through a series of disasters that could have befallen him. Has he set the kitchen on fire? Did he try and squeeze his huge body into the Dumbwaiter? Has he smashed something, broken a chair? Fed Rex the box of hand-made chocolate truffles that were on top of the piano? Has he spilled a hot drink onto the piano keys? Anthony has two left feet and is always crashing into something, and putting his foot in it either verbally or literally. I call him without even listening to the messages – God knows what's happened, I dread to think.

He picks up. "Pearl, thank God."

I can hear outside sounds – sirens, cars, horns, cries. "Anthony, are you on the street?"

"I'm getting into a cab."

"Oh, where are you going? Shopping? Wait for me, I'm on my way home."

"Pearl, I'm catching a flight back to San Francisco. Bruce is ill, it's an emergency."

I roll my eyes. Bruce did this last time. He is incapable of being without his boyfriend for five minutes. Co-dependency does not even begin to describe their ten year relationship. "Anthony, you know what a drama queen Bruce is."

"No, this is an emergency. Seriously. An. Emergency! He's had an aortic aneurism. Something to do with the heart. He's in intensive care. Oh my God, I'm like, freaking out, I think he's going to die," he wails.

A wave of guilt washes over me for my dismissive attitude. "He's not going to die. Calm down – if he's at the hospital they'll get him through this. Have faith, Ant. Stay strong. Why are you taking a cab to the airport? Suresh could have driven you there."

"He was running errands, I couldn't wait."

I hear the cab door slam and the vehicle screech off. "What can I do to help? Do you want me to come with you? I have money – let me sort out the medical bill."

Anthony seems as if he is going to burst into tears. "No and no. There isn't any point you coming and hanging around at the hospital – there's nothing you can do. And Bruce's job has great benefits – he has full insurance. Thanks, anyway, Pearly – I appreciate the offer."

"Well let me know if there's anything you need."

"I will. Shame, I was having such a ball at Alexandre's palace. I mean yours and Alexandre's palace – if only Bruce wasn't afraid of flying and he'd have come too -maybe this would never have happened."

"Life happens when you're busy making plans," I say.

"John Lennon said that."

"Yes, he did. And that was before he got shot. There's nothing you could have done, Anthony. Life throws stuff at you sometimes – things that are beyond your control."

"Shit happens, huh?"

"Exactly," I whisper, thinking of our mom.

"Listen, I've got to go – I need some time to think."

"Good luck, Ant. I'm praying for Bruce. Call me later."

"Bye Pearl." The line goes dead.

I mull over the fragility of our existence. One second everything can be perfect and the next, bam, anything can change and there's not a lot you can do about it.

Except - live each day as if it were your last.

3

I need someone to talk to. Bruce's aneurism has really knocked the wind out of me. Not that I am a huge Bruce fan but he is everything to my brother and I can't bear to see Anthony's life fall apart. It brings it all gushing back again; my mother's unexpected death. You'd think the pain would go away after all these years but that feeling of abandonment never leaves your side – the eternal lurking shadow which accompanies even your happy moods.

Alexandre is still en route to London so I can't talk to him.

I dial my best friend - poor long-suffering Daisy. I say long-suffering because she always talks my problems through with me. That's just the way she is. Even if I try to discuss *her* she somehow swings the conversation back round to me. It's in her nature, and besides, it's her job. At least it *was* before she got married and had a child. She was a full-time counselor cum therapist when she lived in London. Now that little Amy's at school all day, Daisy is back working again. Or will be soon. She has set up an office in the maid's room in her pre-war apartment block. A lot of these old apartments come with small 'box' rooms – that once were maids' quarters in the days when people rang bells for service, had their baths drawn and drinks brought to them. These days, only people like Alexandre live this way. And now me. I still can't get used to the luxury of my new life and feel guilty every time I see his staff running around for us. It doesn't seem right. Indecent, almost. But Patricia gets cross with me if I don't act the complete 'lady'. She winces when I put plates in the dishwasher or begin to scrub a pan. I need to act more like the princess people expect me to be in my privileged situation.

Daisy picks up on the first ring.

"Hi Daisy, it's Pearl, are you busy, am I interrupting anything?"

"Hi gorgeous. Right now, I need to take care of a few calls but my eleven o'clock has just cancelled on me, so come over then."

"You have appointments already? That's fantastic!" I cry out.

"Joel - he's my charity case, I don't charge him a penny," Daisy tells me in her British drawl. "Getting back into the swing of things, you know. But I do have my first paid patient, I mean *client*, coming in next Thursday. Come on over – see my nest-like office. Just got a new couch – it's a bit squeezed but I look pretty professional in my new surroundings."

"Can't wait to check it all out. See you at eleven."

I grab my gym bag where I keep my swimsuit and decide to go for a workout at the pool. I usually do fifty lengths. Gets the lungs working, and the blood pumping – it keeps me in shape. Although Alexandre has installed a gym at his apartment, working out with him is a disaster – I can't concentrate. Apparently, Barack and Michelle Obama exercise together every morning. *Do they work out or just leap on each other?* Because when I see Alexandre pumping those biceps, sweat beading on that toned chest of his, his cute, tight buns clenched in action, all I want to do is jump his bones. No, I need a nice peaceful swimming session *alone* to keep my concentration in check.

Daisy has done wonders with her tiny space. It's intimate but it works. The walls are painted burgundy. I wonder if people will imagine that they are back in their mothers' wombs – safe, protected. It certainly makes you feel you could tell her any inner thought - although Daisy has that effect on people, at least on me. The burgundy clashes with her natural red hair and, as if on purpose, she's donning an orange dress. Very Autumnal. She has two framed certificates of her diplomas on the wall and a photograph on her desk of her daughter Amy and her husband together in an embrace. There's a small library of books on a shelf behind; Freud, Carl Jung and titles like *Stage Theory of Psychosocial Development* and *Eponymous Influences in Therapy*.

"What d'you think?" she asks proudly.

"I think you'll have a line of people clamoring down your door."

"Really? I feel so insecure, you know, I've been out of the picture for ages but Amy's just turned five, is at school all day now and I need to get my independence back."

I lean back on her couch. "My father once gave me a great

piece of advice. He said, 'Pearl, whatever happens, whatever you do, even if you end up with someone wealthy you always need to have your own 'fuck-you' money. Money that's just yours that you can do what you like with. Women need to have their own fuck-you money at all times. You never know when you'll need to catch a plane or treat yourself to something special.' "

Daisy laughs and throws her curly head back and swivels in her therapist's chair. "That's brilliant and so true. That's why I'm doing this! I need 'fuck-you' money, too. I mean, Johnny's very generous and earns enough for us all but if I want to go on a wild underwear splurge at Victoria's Secret or pig out at the gourmet bakery at Dean & DeLuca, that's my prerogative, right? I don't want to feel guilty about it. 'Fuck-you' money, I love it! What about your 'fuck-you' money, Pearl? Do you feel as if Alexandre is being too controlling, still? A couple of weeks ago it seemed to be really bugging you. Is he still pushing you about getting pregnant ASAP?"

"Yes, but it hasn't happened so we'll cross that unlikely bridge if we come to it. The truth is though, I'm relieved I'm not pregnant right now. It would all be too much going on at once."

"What about the wedding date?"

"Alexandre's cooled off a bit about that but just can't understand why I need a bit more time. And he gave in about the company. As far as money goes, I get a generous director's salary from HookedUp Enterprises plus a percentage of any future projects that I orchestrate. It's all been drawn up legally with lawyers. I refused to be given a stake in the company, much to his irritation. If at a later date my projects go well then I can buy in. I want to know I deserve the money I earn."

"Wise. What about your apartment? You're not selling that,

are you?"

"No, I'm subletting. It's a nice, regular income that I can rely on."

"Fuck-you money."

I laugh. "Exactly. Just in case I have to take off running," I joke.

"Good girl. Smart move. You need to keep your autonomy."

"Exactly," I agree. "I don't want hand-outs. I've always earned my own living. Anthony thinks I'm nuts, though."

"Yes, well - he would. I know Anthony's your brother but he's such a wanker. Why are you always so forgiving with him? You've got to face it, he really is pretty cruel to you Pearl."

"I know. He doesn't really mean it though."

Daisy arranges some papers on her desk. "There you go again – always defending him. Do you ever tell him to F off? I wouldn't stand for such continual negativity."

"We had a huge fight once and I did, I told him to get out of my life. Well, guess what? I've never told anyone this, Daisy, but…well, he attempted suicide…took a load of pills, so you can imagine how I felt. It wasn't because of me that he did it, but still."

"Oh, shit. How long ago was this?"

"About two years after John died. So you know, John died of an overdose, my mom died of cancer, I hardly see my dad so…"

"I see. Guilt and fear. Guilt is powerful."

"Anthony is incorrigible. He thinks I should 'snap up Alexandre before he realizes what's happened' – those were his very words. Oh, and become a 'trophy wife'. Do younger men have trophy wives who are older than they are? Don't you have to be arm candy to be a trophy wife?"

"You *are* arm candy, Pearl, believe me. Arm candy with intelligence. Age doesn't stop anyone being beautiful. In fact, I think you look better now than you ever did. And you seem so much more self-possessed lately, not so needy."

"What d'you mean?"

"Well when you first met Alexandre you were practically wetting your knickers over him – sorry I didn't mean that," she bursts out into a cascade of giggles. "No - but I mean you were behaving as if you were the lucky one, completely dismissing the fact that he, too, was getting a great deal."

I put my hand on hers. "Oh, sweetie, you think I'm a great deal?"

"I think you're a *bargain* and he should be bloody grateful. Just because he's loaded and gorgeous and younger than you doesn't make him more special than you are. And you need to be aware of that. The truth is, Pearl, you were behaving like a teenager. I can tell you now because you seem to be pretty much back to normal but I was a little worried for a while. I mean, I know you basically hadn't had any decent sex for twenty years and never thought you'd meet anyone ever again, so I do understand why you went so gaga over him, but still, he really had you under his thumb."

Little does she know, I think, and find myself humming *Under My Thumb* again, remembering what Alexandre did with his magic touch. Is still *doing* with his magic touch.

"Yes, but he wasn't aware of my Jell-O insides," I say. "One of the reasons he was attracted to me was that I was 'mature'. Luckily, because of your wise advice of acting 'cool, calm and collected' he wasn't party to my insecure, self-doubting internal dialogue or I think he would have dumped me."

Daisy arches her delicate eyebrows. "You worry about that a lot, don't you? Desertion. Being dumped…left in the lurch?"

I tell Daisy about the whole Bruce saga, how I fear for Anthony, and how it has triggered the dread of abandonment and loneliness – memories of my mother's sudden death. Then I add, "I don't want to go into this marriage for the wrong reasons. I want Alexandre to really know me and love me for *me* – the good the bad and the ugly."

To my amazement, Daisy takes Anthony's side on this topic and warns, "Be careful, Pearl, he's a Latin man at heart. I'm speaking as your friend, you understand – professionally I'd probably urge you to be completely honest, but you're not my client, you're my best mate. Latin men can be jealous and possessive – believe me I know, I dated one. They have that virgin/whore complex going on. I really, *really* would think twice about coming clean about divulging sexual history – there are some things better left unsaid."

I bite my lip. Maybe she's right. Although, the truth is I had blanked it all out. I can't even remember, anyway.

She goes on, "You don't want him to know about what happened that time. He really doesn't need to be privy to it all–"

"But I was a different person then."

"You were cocky and sassy and brimming with self-confidence – you were only twenty-two."

"Exactly," I agree, remembering how I then didn't suffer from insecurities - that at that age I felt I owned the world.

"Still, best to keep it all under wraps, don't you think? Let sleeping dogs lie," she advises.

I cross my legs almost in self defense. "It's a blur, anyway, Daisy. I genuinely can't remember what happened but it *is* a part of me still, whether I like it or not. I suppose I just feel like really opening up to Alexandre, that's all. I don't want us to hold secrets from each other."

Daisy strokes my cheek and brushes a tendril of hair away from my eye. "You want to talk about it, how it messed everything up with Brad…empty your heart and soul, re-open painful wounds? That's fine - I totally get that, me more than anyone. But talk to *me* about it, or any other close friend, or even another therapist - I could recommend a colleague to you - but your future husband who happens to be a proud Frenchman? I'm thinking, no, bad idea, or you could really screw things up. Look, maybe I'm wrong and totally overreacting; maybe he'd be understanding, adorable and wouldn't give a toss. But I'm just speaking from my own personal experience. It's up to you, Pearl, but my gut feeling is this: he's crazy about you – he thinks you're perfect. Why risk jeopardizing that?"

"I guess you could be right," I mumble.

There's an awkward silence and then Daisy says enthusiastically, "On a brighter note – tell me about your wedding dress; have you chosen the designer yet? Let me know if you want me to come along and help you pick something out."

"I forgot to tell you, Daisy – it's all arranged. Zang Toi is doing my gown."

"You're joking? But won't that cost a fortune? You told me you didn't want Alexandre paying for your dress and I know your father doesn't have a bean. I read somewhere that Zang Toi dresses like…Saudi princesses…and Bill Gates's wife – *that's* when he's not too busy with the likes of Eva Longoria and Sharon Stone."

"He does, but Sophie's paying. It's her wedding gift to me.

She has insisted and won't take no for an answer. Zang Toi was *her* idea."

Daisy goes white. You. Are. Kidding. Me."

"No, really, she's being as sweet as pie at the moment."

"And you trust that?"

I grimace. "No, but what am I meant to do? Tell her she's a scheming bitch and that I suspect her of foul play? If she insists on spending sixty-three thousand dollars on me and it makes Alexandre happy and I'm going to get the most stunning wedding gown in the whole wide world, then who am I to disagree?"

"*Sixty-three thousand dollars??* But that's insane money! I know Sophie and Alexandre are loaded but—"

"Alexandre," I interrupt, "is rich and powerful but Sophie? Oh my God, that woman has her money invested everywhere - Vegas and half way round the United States and Latin America, and Lord knows where else. She *oozes* wealth. Alexandre spends his money on cars and property, but her? She *invests*. She plays the stock market. Who knows what pies her bony fingers are stuck into but I wouldn't be surprised if she's involved with Russian mafia or something. I know sixty-three thousand is a fortune for you and me, but for Sophie it's not even a morning's work."

Daisy presses her thumb up to her lips in thought. "Hmm, I wonder what her plan is. Maybe, knowing she's going to be your sister-in-law has made her turn over a new leaf and the wedding dress is her peace offering."

"You think?"

Daisy sniggers. "No, not for a second, I was being sarcastic. I think she could be plotting and scheming something. Watch out."

"Me too. I mean, I'd love to believe that she genuinely wants to be friends - of course - but my little voice inside tells me not to trust her."

"If I were you, I'd listen to that little voice." Daisy narrows her eyes. "I smell a rat."

I saunter through Central Park on my way back to the office, taking my time, mulling over what Daisy has said. I think of Sophie and her dark past, how she worked as a prostitute when she was only seventeen. Alexandre never judged her for that and even got angry with me when I made a benign comment. So how then, would he judge me for one thing that happened in my past? Would he think less of me? Would it spoil everything? Both Daisy and Anthony seem to think it's not worth the risk. But Alexandre is a forgiving person. He'd love me anyway.

Or would he? Perhaps things are better left unsaid.

The day's still beautiful. I take out my iPod and find *Autumn in New York* and put on my headset– what song could be more perfect? I have on my lightweight sneakers, which - as any New Yorker knows - is part and parcel of living in this city - walking is one of the great pleasures of living here. I kick up the crispy, golden leaves as squirrels scatter in front of me. I observe them leap up boughs of American Elm trees; a variety which has been decimated all through its range by the ravages of Dutch elm disease, but miraculously still alive and thriving in Central Park.

I feel the warmth of sun on my back; the sky is crystal blue. There are people sprawled on park benches reading newspapers, Smartphone texting and snoozing in the morning rays. Dogs are charging about trying their luck with a squirrel catch. I regret that

Rex isn't with me. Dogs complete a real walk. I decide to pass by the apartment to collect Rex and take him to the office. He loves hanging out there and is a star amongst the staff; his treat every now and then to come to work and lap up the attention they lavish on him – his white cravat of a chest stroked, his ears caressed. I'll order something in for lunch – some Chinese perhaps – I have a lot of work to catch up on, and Natalie needed a second opinion about a project she's working on.

I'm singing along to *Autumn in New York* and making a mental list when I feel the buzz of my cell. I fumble about for it and pick up.

The voice is familiar but I don't recognize it straight away. I switch off my iPod so I can hear better.

"Pearl?"

"Speaking."

"Sam."

"Oh, hi Sam." Samuel Myers – that was fast. Such a quick answer can mean only one thing. A 'no' to my proposal.

"Lunch?"

"Oh, okay." I look at my watch. Lunch is now.

"You sound surprised," he snorts.

Uh, oh - the cool, sophisticated woman in the chic suit is now wearing sneakers, has damp mussed-up hair from swimming and is in a twisted mess of iPod wires tangled all over her head. I take a neat breath. "No, Sam, not surprised at all. I would love to do lunch. In fact, it'll be my treat. How about the Century Club?"

He chuckles. "The Century? You're a member? Too stuffy. Where are you right now?"

"In Central Park at about Sixty Third, or so."

"I'll book a table at Daniel. Is that good for you, sweetheart?"

"It's my local haunt but it's closed at lunch time."

I hear him breathing heavily. "Oh, darn. Let's just meet at The Plaza, then. Meet me there in… twenty minutes, say – in the restaurant at The Palm Court."

I start sprinting. I need to get there fast before he does – empty out my monstrous bag of tricks in the ladies' room and transform myself into the glamorous ball-breaking executive I was just a few hours before.

I emerge fresh from the powder room at The Plaza, looking composed and primed, and as sleek as a panther on the hunt. High heels back on, suit smoothed out, hair in a chignon bun, make-up perfect, just a touch of lip gloss.

Samuel Myers has something up his sleeve, I can be sure of that, or he would have just called, not suggested a lunch meeting. Or does he just want to get into my panties? Ha! Some chance. He's used to bimbos in LA - pretty young actresses who'll do anything for a break. He's fat and balding but he's powerful; the strongest aphrodisiac of them all for a lot of females. Not me, though. Money doesn't motivate me. Even if Alexandre had been a bus boy I would have fallen for him anyway.

The maitre'd shows me to our table, and to my amazement Samuel Myers is already seated, eagerly waiting for me. The room is massive, bordered with mirrored arched windows all around and fleur-de-pêche marbled columns. This airy room's crowning glory is a stained-glass yellow and green skylight way up high – the restored 1907 décor is breathtaking. Funny, how when you live in a city you neglect its best landmarks. I haven't set foot in The Plaza for years.

I find Samuel almost hidden behind a potted palm tree beaming at me.

"Pearl - we meet again," he says in a motion to get up, although he plunks himself right back down in his chair with the effort.

"Sam," I say, shaking his hand heartily.

"Not the most elegant cuisine in the city but there are some nice organic things on the Eloise menu. I can report back to my wife that I'm being a good boy and sticking to my diet."

"Diets are tough," I say. "Actually, I've never managed more than three hours of being on a diet."

He snorts with laughter. "I don't believe that for a minute, Pearl. You're so svelte, so slim and trim."

"I cheat."

"Oh yes? How?" he asks eagerly.

"I swim a lot. It's amazing what you can get away with when you go for the burn."

He sounds disappointed and says in a glum tone, "I wish I could admit to doing the same but I'm a lazy old man with a sweet tooth and a penchant for Cognac."

I suppress a grin. The waiter comes and we both order. The swim has given me an appetite so I ask for organic grilled chicken, mashed potato, carrots and sweet peas. Sam orders a hot dog.

"So should we get down to business?" he breathes.

My heart starts racing but I smile serenely, wondering what's in store.

"You got me thinking, Pearl. A lot. And I want to meet you

half way.

"You do?" I ask, wondering where this is leading.

"You say Thelma and Louise. I say, just Thelma. No Louise. Because the other part needs to go to a guy. I need box office. I need testosterone. I'm obliged to hire a star which means I have to go easy on the budget – like I said before, I can't have two big names. That's where your Thelma comes in. The guy and the girl. A buddy movie with a twist."

I cross my legs, hold my hand up to my chin and listen intently. "Go on."

"What's the name of that woman who won a Tony Award for that play, *Seeking Sandrine* – the half-Italian actress? She was good."

"Alessandra Demarr."

He shakes his head. "Forget it. I've heard she's gay."

"So? She's a great actress. Even better if she's gay - we'd see the character from a different angle – it could really deepen the story. I mean, whatever happens, the script is going to need some more tweaking."

He ponders this and says, "I guess the advantage is that she won't be too expensive and the whole gay thing she's got going could work in our favor. The two leads can play off each other. Flirt but not get involved, you know. I like it, actually. I like it a lot."

"I had a feeling about you, Sam," I flatter him, "I knew you'd *get* it."

"My wife likes the idea of a female lead. My daughter *loves* the idea. We could be onto a winner here."

"And if Alessandra Demarr's not free?"

"Oh, she'll be free all right. Her agent will be chomping at the bit, guaranteed. Leave it to me, I'll sort it out."

"Really? That simple?"

"I have to leave for LA tonight but I'll set up a meeting. You two can get together next week or the week after."

"LA or New York?"

"Take your pick, sweetheart. You decide."

I look up at the glass ceiling and ponder my options. New York or Los Angeles? "I'll talk it over with my fiancé," I tell him, and imagine that a little trip with Alexandre might just be the tonic.

4

I've been parted from Alexandre for less than twelve hours yet I still ache with his absence. I had gotten so used to living alone before I met him that it seemed normal to be doing everything solo, save a dinner here or there with Daisy or with a group of friends. All I did was work. Now I'm part of a busy household, loved by a fiancé who calls me every few hours and I even have a dog. Everything has changed - I wonder how I survived before.

The day has been so full-on with those two meetings with Samuel Myers, swimming and Daisy that I'm now soaking in the tub with some magazines, a glass of wine and some great chill-out music - *Play* by Funk. Heaven. Made all the sweeter by Anthony's call to me earlier - Bruce has been stabilized, the operation was a success and he's going to be okay. Panic over. I'm searching online on my iPad for hotels in Los Angeles when a Skype call comes through from Alexandre.

"Hi baby," I say and wait for the video to come on. His handsome face appears on the screen and my stomach gives a little lurch. I can't believe that still, every time I see that face, or wake up with him next to me, it's as if I'm setting eyes on him for the very first time.

"Hey sexy," he says, his voice deep, his eyes heavy-lidded. You're in the bath?"

"Had a busy, very eventful day."

"Sorry, I couldn't call earlier – was in that fucking meeting forever."

"And?"

"All good. Sophie ate them alive. We're going to do extremely well with this. Got an edge on any future competition – got the British government eating out of our hands."

I think of how Alexandre promised me that he would sell his share of HookedUp to Sophie and concentrate on starting new projects of his own, but now I realize that may never happen. He and his sister are as entwined as ivy in this business together. It seems he needs her on some deep, psychological level. But I don't want to nag him on this issue so I have said very little lately. Especially as she's being so sugar-sweet to me - I really don't have a leg to stand on.

"What about you?" he continues, his eyes scanning my naked shoulders soothed with big white, foamy suds from the bubble bath.

"Well, after that little porn film that you whipped up this morning, right in the middle of my million-dollar meeting, thank-you-very-much, dear fiancé, I have to say it was a little tricky to concentrate, but Samuel Myers and I have made a deal."

Alexandre smirks irreverently; his wicked mouth a little

crooked making a tiny dimple appear in his cheek. "I knew you'd handle it. Nothing can faze you, Pearl, not even my dick."

I laugh. "Of course Samuel Myers is delighted. He really enjoyed your video – thinks you could be a big star. He's branching out into doing porn movies and would like to sign you."

Alexandre's face flinches for a second but then breaks into a broad grin. "Very funny."

"No, but seriously, the meeting went better than expected. Two meetings, actually. We've got Alessandra Demarr on board," I tell him proudly. "An LA trip could be coming up shortly."

"Really, you're joking – Alessandra Demarr?"

A rush of surprise courses through my body. "You know who she is?"

"Of course I do. I saw her at the National in a play. She's an amazing actress - stunning too - she looks like a young Sophia Loren."

I smile sweetly but feel nauseous inside. *Why am I jealous? It's absurd.* Perhaps it's because I'm blonde and girl-next-door-ish and Alessandra Demarr is a ravishing beauty – the type that screams sex-siren and smoldering sophistication. "She's gay," I snap, not meaning the words to come out that way.

"So I've heard. Nothing like a sexy gay woman to turn a man on."

"You're *attracted* to her," I hear my voice creak out. I try to stay cool – after all, he can see every expression on my face, every nuance of emotion.

"I'm attracted to you, baby, and I know you have a penchant for pretty women. That first time, in your apartment, when you told me the story of your first real orgasm when your best friend stroked you with a feather? That was the sexiest thing I'd ever heard. Fuck, I'm hard now just thinking about it."

"I'd love to suck your cock right now," I purr, making sure he has *me* on his brain and not Alessandra Demarr. I know I'm going to have to keep him well away from her. Gay people can be swung and I'd rather not put temptation in his path.

"Tell me what you'd do," he says, running his tongue along his upper lip. His thickly lashed eyes sear into me – tiger's eyes – keen, intense as if he wants to eat me whole.

"First, I'd take your big, beautiful cock in both hands and bury my head between your legs," I murmur. "I'd run your silky smoothness around my nose, my cheeks and then on my lips, breathing in the smell of you, and just run my eyes all over you – this one thousand percent pure, unadulterated all-male, luscious helping of Alexandre Chevalier."

His lips tip up in that crooked smile of his.

And I keep talking, "I'd tease my lips along your balls and gently flick them with the tip of my tongue, letting it ride up your length - your thick, throbbing cock – thinking about how it's gonna make me come after I'm done with sucking it first – how it's so sexy and virile that even after that big bad boy has spurted in my mouth, it's ready again for round two."

He groans. "Always ready for another round with you, Pearl. Always ready to fuck your slick, wet, tight pearlette."

I smile at his poetic rhyme and continue, "I'll ring my tongue around your soft, satiny head, making it flicker over your one-eyed jack. I'll slowly lick off your pre-cum – you always taste so good, so sweet, Alexandre. The only man in the world I could ever do that to."

"Don't even put the idea of another man into my head," he

growls. "I don't want to know who's touched you - I don't even want to *imagine* you having ever been with anyone else. Your *mine,* do you hear that, Pearl? You're *mine* - and you were born to be mine."

I instantly regret what I've said – it's made him edgy. His gaze narrows – his green eyes on fire, covetous, greedy for me. I know I have to keep my secrets to myself or all hell could break loose – I can't risk letting him find out anything. But it turns me on – knowing his jealous flame is alight. My Venus is pounding with desire – I squeeze my thighs tightly together as both hands are holding onto my tablet and I don't want to drop it in the bath. That already happened a couple of weeks ago with this very same scenario – Sex-Skyping is getting to be a regular habit with us. I'm writhing now, squeezing, crossing my legs and clenching myself. I need this release.

"I want you to come in my mouth," I carry on in a whisper.

"Tomorrow night I'll be back and I'm gonna lick you all over, tease your clit – then I'll fuck you. Your. Tight. Wet. Pearlette is going to Make. Me. Explode."

"Alexandre, I'll be with you in a minute." I can't bear it anymore. I set the iPad down on the floor and turn on the faucet of the shower-head. I can hear him moaning now, groaning at the release of his orgasm. I think of his gorgeous face, his dark hair flopping about his defined cheekbones, his huge, smooth cock stretching me open and fucking me. I turn up the power of the water and let it pound my clit. I press the metal on my mound and it's enough to push me to the edge – the water's firing inside my slit, shooting at my clitoris like tiny bullets – I start climaxing in a shattering orgasm, rushing through me with continual spasms as the water continues to draw out the intensity of pleasure; my sensitive core coming in undulating waves.

I finally let go of the shower head.

I reach down for my tablet and observe the relaxed face of Alexandre, spent, orgasmed-out, but then my freaking battery goes dead. I set the iPad back down. I lie back in the bath and press my fingers on my clit to draw out the last little ripples of satisfaction.

I close my eyes and snooze off, the warm water lapping around me in a gentle swell.

I was looking hot. Really hot. Loved getting ready to go out. Madonna's latest hit, *Secret*, was playing on the radio and I was moving my hips to the rhythm, dancing around the room. I checked myself again in the mirror and tossed my teased-up curls about and then ran my fingers through my long, wild blonde hair. Eyes looking like smoldering fires – make-up just right. At least *some* guys appreciated me. Fuck him! Fuck Brad – I'll show him. He needs *space*, I'll show him goddam space.

We'd been dating for four years and now, suddenly, he was telling me he needed space! I knew it was because of his studies, I knew - med school looming, exams to get through. That, I could understand, but all that studying lately with Alicia – all those all-nighters. I'm not some Kleenex to be tossed aside, I'm your girlfriend, I told myself. He didn't want me to cramp his style? Two can play at that game, buddy.

Julia breezed into my dorm. "Are you ready?"

"What d'you think?"

"I think your skirt might be a little short," she said eyeing up my electric-blue mini, my legs going on forever in high, clunky heels.

I laughed. "If you've got it, flaunt it."

"You don't usually wear stuff so…so *revealing*," she stammered.

"I want to look sexy."

"You always look sexy, Pearl, you don't need to try so hard."

"*All I wanna do, is have some fun,*" I sang.

"Come on Sheryl Crow, or we'll be late. The boys said to meet them at the bar."

"*So* not my thing," I said, rolling my eyes, "football, frat boys from that dorky college but, hey, who knows? Maybe we'll have a good time."

I wake up with a jolt. The bath water's tepid. I must have dozed off. I bury my hands in my face as hot tears pool in my eyes. Memories are being unleashed but I'm not sure why. All this talk lately about keeping my past to myself is making me remember.

I let the plug out and stand up. I grab a warm towel and relish the cocoon feeling it gives me when I wrap it tightly about my cold body. I wish Alexandre were here. I need him. I need his strong arms to protect me, to envelop me with love.

I'd completely forgotten about that electric-blue skirt.

I get out of the tub, take another towel and dry my feet. My tablet's on the floor and I take it back to the bedroom and plug it in. The cell is sitting on the bed – I pick it up and call.

"I just want to hear your voice," I tell my husband-to-be but it's just his voicemail. *Where can he be?* I flop on the bed, slip under the down comforter and before I know it I've lapsed into a profound sleep.

I was leaning against the juke box – lapping up everybody's stares – all eyes were on me and my sexy dance moves. I'd lost count of how many shots of tequila I'd had. I was licking the salt seductively off my lips, then I tilted my head back to empty yet another glass. The blond guy – what was his name – he had his hand up my electric-blue mini; the other was fisting my hair. The music was loud – Snoop Doggy Dog singing intensely about something intense. The football player shouted in my ear, "Fuck, you're hotter than a bitch in heat," and then he said to his friend, "we all need to get out of here."

I'm suddenly in a lavender field and Alexandre is smiling at me. "Don't worry, baby, you're with me now. I won't let anything happen to you."

"But it already *has* happened," I say. "It's too late."

I wake up with a start and feel the small of my back drenched with sweat. The bottom sheet is soaked. I peel off my silk nighty, toss it, and shift my naked body over to a fresh part of the bed. Blurry-eyed, I look at my watch. Two twenty-five a.m. I swivel it around; it's a Reverso, (another extravagant gift from Alexandre) and the other face, the London-time side, says seven twenty-five – five hours ahead. Perhaps Alexandre is having breakfast; like a true Parisian, drinking a strong dark espresso. Should I call? And say what? My dreams are keeping me awake but I can't tell you what they are.

As if he could smell my angst, Rex comes wagging into the room. His basket is next to the kitchen but he comes to say good morning every day. Today he's five hours early. He nuzzles his nose next to my hand which is dangling over the mattress. Dogs know when things aren't right – they *know*.

"Alright, Rex, but don't tell Daddy - come on up."

He gazes up at me with his almond-shaped eyes as if to say, "Really? Truly?"

I'll get in trouble for this. Rex isn't allowed on the bed but I'm sad and lonely, so who cares. I pat the mattress and he jumps up excitedly, his windmill tail in motion, digging his paws into the comforter, not believing his luck. Tomorrow, I'll change the sheets so there's no evidence. He crawls almost on top of me and I put my arms about his solid black body and squeeze him tight. "Just this once Rex, as a special treat – I could really use a hug right now," and I kiss his soft, silky ears. I need him close to get through the night. He's my bodyguard to chase away the bad dreams.

I fall fast asleep with my doggie-love in my arms.

"Ah, ha! Caught you, you naughty boy!"

I rouse from my sleep and there's a big commotion going on around me, Rex padding about the bed, wild with happiness. Alexandre has tried to sneak into the bedroom without waking me but got more than he bargained for.

I look at my watch - 7a.m. "You're back early," I mumble into my pillow, my eyes half closed.

"I wanted to surprise you," he replies, planting a soft kiss on my lips, "but it looks as if you got there first - while the cat's away—"

"I couldn't sleep – I needed a French lover by my side. You were gone so Rex offered himself up."

Just then, I hear the elevator door open and Rex leaps off the bed and into the hallway. Sally must have arrived to take him on his morning walk. I rouse from my sleepiness and stretch my arms languidly in the air. "I've missed you, Alexandre."

He throws his raincoat on a chair. "Next time I go, you're coming with me. I don't like us being separated." He moves towards me, his eyes flashing with passion. He strokes my head and then folds me in his strong arms, pressing his face to my throat and breathing me in as if his life depended on it.

"I felt empty without you," I whisper. I relax into him, his natural scent is intoxicating, and my heart beats with anxiety at the thought of being away from him again. Ridiculous; it's been less than two days. I bury my head in his wide, warm chest. He lifts my chin with his hand for a kiss but I slip away from his clutch. "I'll be back, hang on a sec," I tell him, sidling underneath his embrace.

"Meanwhile, I'm getting straight into bed," he says.

I go to the bathroom to pee, freshen up and brush my teeth. When Alexandre tried to kiss me just now I closed my mouth tightly, lips sealed – morning breath, the horror of it. Why is it I always want to be perfect for him? I want to be his princess – faultless, blameless and flawless. I want to reach unattainable heights. Yet at the very same time, I yearn for him to love me just the way I am and for all my faults, even my wrong doings. A paradox. I'm asking for the impossible.

When my teeth are squeaky clean and I've washed my private parts in the wonderful bidet that Alexandre had specially installed, I feel ready to come back to bed. I stand at the bathroom door and just survey the scene around me, realizing that my luck is a chance in a million. How many people get to love someone in their lives? I mean, really fall in love, not because of habit, or convenience or security but for passion – get to experience a real romance? I observe him now lying in bed and imagine there must have been angels fluttering about me that day when I bumped into him at the coffee shop four months ago. Was Cupid there, himself, with his bow and arrow? What were the odds of that?

Was Puck from *A Midsummer Night's Dream* sprinkling love dust in Alexandre's eyes?

Because what were the chances that a ravishing, twenty-five year-old Frenchman with the world at his feet would fall in love with a run-of-the-mill, forty year-old American woman?

"What are you staring at?" he asks with a grin.

"You."

"You're so beautiful, Pearl. Even when you're all ruffled up and half asleep – especially when you're ruffled up. You're like a fluffy chick, all sweet and innocent. Come here, I need to hold you."

I scurry over and slip under the comforter. Nestling myself next to him, I wonder where he gets these notions that I'm so unblemished. If he knew otherwise, would he do a one hundred and eighty degree turn?

He takes me in his arms again and strokes my hair. "You're

my jewel, my angel – your hair's like spun gold in this morning light."

I run my fingers underneath his T-shirt; I need to feel him, to own his flesh and blood, press my fingers against his heartbeat to make sure this is all real. He lifts up his arms and I ease the T-shirt over his strong shoulders and fix my eyes on the rise and fall of his pecs moving with the rhythm of his breath. I touch his smooth skin and marvel at the fact that this gorgeous man before me is going to be my husband.

He gazes at me for a moment, his green eyes tender and warm, and then rests his defined lips on mine, softly at first. Then his tongue begins to tease me, running quietly along my upper lip. I let my mouth open and close my eyes in response. My tongue meets his and the tips tantalize each other in little flutters, like wings of a humming bird above a flower full of nectar; quivering, flickering. I moan and grip my arms tightly about his shoulders – I can't be near enough to him – close enough – this is beyond desire; it is an aching need for Alexandre to own me, to possess me. I abandon myself to him completely. I tilt my head back and melt into him; relaxed like a rag doll as his lips devour me, wet and all-consuming into a deep, insatiable kiss - our mouths as one, our tongues tangled in love and want for each other. I pull back for a beat to catch my breath, then nip his bottom lip playfully and open my eyes to observe his all-male beauty.

"I love you, Pearl. I need you." He pulls me into him and cups his hand under my butt forcing me even nearer. I feel his solid erection up against my belly and a bolt of desire shoots between my legs making me moan again. He licks my tongue with fiery lashes, the passion growing as if this kiss were alive - a being with a heart and soul all of its own. "You're mine, Pearl," he growls like an untamed panther. "Only mine – you have never belonged to anyone else – you were made for me, God created you just for *me*."

I pull myself up a little higher so that his erection is poised at my entrance. "I've been waiting for you my whole life, even when I didn't know it," I breathe through the kiss. "All my unhappiness, my loneliness before I met you was so I'd know what it was to really feel loved. You can't appreciate true love until you've been in a desert, looked Despair in the eyes. I don't want to be like that ever again."

"I'll never let you go, I promise."

A hot tear trickles down my cheek and Alexandre licks it before it falls. We're now lying side by side and I feel him enter me slowly. I gasp. My Venus is throbbing, my nipples hard and rosy. He thrusts himself into me and I cry out at the surprise.

His eyes flutter half closed in ecstatic reverie and he murmurs, "Jesus, you're so tight but so warm and juicy - coupled with that kiss - I think I'm gonna come." He holds his hips still. I can feel the pulse of his cock flexing inside me, stretching me, blood pumping through his taut veins, filling my walls – but he doesn't come, he has too much self-control. "I don't want to fuck you," he whispers, "I want us to make love." I sense myself shudder at the deliciousness of his lips grazing against my ear, sending shivers all through my body.

He may have self-control but I don't. The shaft of his penis is rubbing delicately against my clit and I start to make little circles tilting upward with my pelvis, my arms hooked about his neck. I can feel it building – the double pleasure of his huge girth inside me pushing all the right places – still motionless – and my clit rubbing against the thick base of his penis - pushing me to my limits.

Then Alexandre starts licking my tongue again in slow swipes and under my tongue, too, at its sensitive root….faster now - little flicks as if he's fucking me with it. The sensation is exquisite. My clit is tingling like a thousand little bells – as if there's a golden thread linking it to my nipples and tongue. Never has a kiss been so sensual. He then presses his thumb on that little space just behind the base of my entrance and I climax in a shudder, riding myself up and down his huge cock, the only movement made by my own friction – he's still motionless. I'm moaning. He clasps both of his large hands around my buttocks and pulls me on top of him in one smooth movement - "That's right baby, ride that orgasm all the way - ride my big, hard, throbbing cock." I'm still climaxing around him when he lunges at me from his position underneath. "Pearl–"

"Alexandre," I moan. I can feel the zealous spurt of him shoot inside me, squirting into my depths in a hot fountain of desire. Both of us are as one – an extension of that kiss now melded into an orgasmic zenith of emotion.

Fucking is great but making love is even better. And that is what I feel emanating from Alexandre's psyche, his soul – the force and power of pure Love with a capital L.

We stay like this for a long time. He's still hard inside me but relaxed as miniscule ripples fade little by little contracting deep inside me. His breath is on mine; he's still looking into my eyes – the orgasm spent but the love surrounding us like a halo of light. No words are needed for how we both feel. I can behold it in his gaze and my core is flashing with a radiant energy from within. I am alive. If I were to die right now I would have tasted Heaven on Earth. My gentle smile creeps into a grin paired with my teary eyes. My emotions are raw and so are his. Like me, he is vulnerable. He, too, has misty eyes but a smile is also dancing on his lips.

We are united in every way.

The essence of true love.

5

A week has gone by, both of us busy with work but having lunch every day together and then meeting up later at home where we usually order something in for dinner. In New York City you are spoiled for choice; whether it be Thai, Indian, Chinese, Mexican or Japanese - even Ethiopian; you name it, you can get the best of it all in Manhattan. Sometimes, Alexandre whips up something mouth-watering himself. He has a knack with any type of cuisine, but especially French and Italian. Alexandre's chef, Vincent, is on vacation.

I need to start getting used to saying things like, 'our chef' and 'our apartment' but it's still taking a while for it all to sink in. Also, this is not my money paying for all this luxury so I find it difficult to use the word 'we' when it concerns 'necessities' that most human beings live quite happily without.

Alexandre set up a mini movie theatre in the apartment so we get to watch movies on the big screen and eat popcorn. Occasionally, Sophie's step-daughter Elodie comes over, still painfully shy and only just eighteen. Alexandre refuses to speak French with her so she's learning fast. He's also paying for her to have private English lessons, so movie night is extra tuition as far as he's concerned – nothing like a good film to make you absorb a language. With a head on her shoulders for anything technical and frighteningly nerdy, Elodie is being groomed as a future heiress to HookedUp – at least that is how it appears to me, although it's unspoken. Alexandre even wants her to spend some time working with me. He's set her up in a pretty apartment in Greenwich Village. He suspects that she rarely goes out and neither of us has seen any evidence of her making friends, hence the choice of Greenwich Village; he thought it would be the right ambience for her to mingle and meet people. So far, she seems to keep to herself, though.

Anthony was right. I feel like Kate Middleton must have felt preparing for her big day. The thought of Sophie spending $63,000 on my wedding gown brings goose-bumps to my flesh. She's an old client of the Malaysian-born designer, Zang Toi – a star who dresses stars and who's been based in New York for the last thirty years or so. I was nervous at first but then I met him and knew straight away that he was special. He's adorable with an infectious laugh and a sense of humor that brings out the child in you. Like many Chinese people, he looks way younger than his fifty-one years. The first time I saw a photo of him he was wearing a mini kilt. Now he usually goes about in a black suit.

Today, I'm off for my first fitting at his showroom, an atelier on Fifty Seventh Street, just a few blocks over from HookedUp Enterprises. He has already promised me that I'll look like a princess on my wedding day. When I saw some of his designs, both vintage and new, I knew that he was right. He's a genius.

I take the elevator up to his floor and am greeted by one of his assistants, a sweet, unassuming girl who could be a teenager but no doubt isn't – those Asian, wrinkle-free genes again. She ushers me into his showroom where there are floor to ceiling windows overlooking Fifty Seventh Street below, and rows of to-die-for gowns and outfits draped from hangers. There is a large desk in the center of the room where he is sitting, his blue-black glossy head bent, busy and in deep concentration. I've heard that he's a shrewd businessman as well as an artist – he learned from a young age, helping out in his parents' grocery store when he was just a boy. He is the seventh child and his lucky number, Sophie told me, is thirteen.

He looks up from his task, rakes his eyes over me quickly and smiles, saying, "You are making my life very easy, Pearl, you're perfect sample size, so no snacking before your wedding!"

I laugh but know he's probably serious. This is not going to be the type of dress to favor a last-minute nip and tuck. "Tell me, Zang, what do you envision for me?" I ask, kissing him on both cheeks. Somehow a handshake seems too formal for such a friendly person.

"I have planned for you a floor length ivory, silk velvet cape with dramatic train and ice crystal beaded blossoms cascading down from the shoulder, and matching strapless gown with ice crystal beaded blossoms cascading up the dramatic flared hem."

"Wow, it sounds beautiful."

"You will be the perfect ice-princess for your handsome French prince," he says with a giggle.

We spend the afternoon discussing the design and all the

different options for shoes. He has me there like a manikin, being draped with muslin cloth, pins going here and there - the fabric itself, the silk velvet, will not be touched until later. He loves the idea of a winter wedding in Lapland and asks me a hundred questions about what food and drink will be served – but even *I'm* not sure about that yet - this is all stuff I have to decide with the wedding planner.

Elodie, of course, will be my maid of honor – she has yet to come in for her fitting, but slim as a pencil, I'm sure Zang will love her – no chance of her pigging out before December; she's like a little waif. With her long brown hair styled with crystal beads, Zang is confident he can transform her into a character from a fairytale.

I leave late, bubbling with excitement and hope – Zang's giggly demeanor is catching and I'm in the highest of spirits.

That's until the elevator door to his showroom opens and Sophie is standing there with a fixed grin on her face.

My heart sinks.

She looks ravishing, impeccable - but then Sophie is always impeccable. She's wearing her thick dark hair loose, the cut chic with Parisian perfection. Her pinstripe pantsuit is tailored. I instantly feel straggly and unkempt next to her mature sophisticated demeanor, even though she's five years younger than I am.

"Pearl, *darling*," she says in her heavy French accent and air-kisses me on both cheeks.

"Sophie, what a lovely surprise, how long are you in town for?"

"Didn't Alexandre tell you I was coming?"

"He must have, but I guess I lost track of time," I lie. I don't want to give her the satisfaction of knowing I fear her and that Alexandre is keeping anything from me. No, he did not let me know she was coming to New York.

I smile sweetly. I feel like the two of us are in that scene from Oscar Wilde's *The Importance of Being Earnest* – two women's saccharine smiles and sweet-talk hiding dagger-like intentions. Although *my* only intention is to avoid her as much as possible. What her plans are for me, I still cannot begin to guess. Except I'm sure they include ousting me from her brother's life in whatever way possible.

She says excitedly, "I thought I'd pop by and see what Zang has designed for Elodie."

"Sophie, I can't thank you enough for this generous gift. I mean, you're really pulling out all the stops."

"Pearl, you're going to be my sister-in-law. Part of my life. If you make Alexandre happy, zat's all I care about." She wrinkles her nose cutely and I wonder, for a second, if she can twitch it like Samantha on *Bewitched* - something I practiced as a child watching endless re-runs on TV - but never mastered. I wouldn't put it past Sophie to be able to come up with a few sorceress tricks, or to cast some sort of wicked spell on me.

Or am I being unjust? Maybe her intentions are good and I'm just a jaded, unforgiving bitch.

Time will tell.

I go back to the office to work and when I get home I find Alexandre on the roof terrace with Rex.

"Hi Pearl, darling," he says, "come and sit on my knee. I'm just finishing up a couple of things." He's tapping away distractedly on his tablet, making lists.

I run my fingers through his thick dark hair and tell him, "I bumped into Sophie at Zang's showroom. You never told me she was coming to New York."

"Sophie's here, in Manhattan?"

"Yes, didn't you know? She said you knew."

"I can't remember her telling me, no."

"Oh," I say, wondering which one of them is fibbing. Sophie, no doubt.

As if the Devil herself were listening in on our conversation, Alexandre's cell rings. I can tell it's Sophie by the way he talks – not just because he's speaking French but the easy expression on his face; the relaxed way you speak to an old friend. My French is getting better every day, namely by hearing him chat on the phone. They're discussing dinner. Great. Just when I was feeling more at ease than ever, our lives perfect, Sophie has to nuzzle in on us. I tense. Is Alexandre now telling her, that yes, I will make dinner tonight? Please, God, no. He knows cooking is not my forte. He ends the conversation and looks at me, his slightly crooked smile showing a hint of irony.

"Did I hear right?" I ask him. "Did you just tell Sophie that I'd cook supper?"

"She asked especially. She wants to taste typical, homemade, American food."

"Well, there are a lot of restaurants that do it way better than I do."

"Nonsense, your cooking is great."

Little does Alexandre know that it's Dean & DeLuca's and

Zabar's cooking which is great, or our local delicatessen. Not me.

He brushes a lock of hair from my face. "Make your hamburgers, they're delicious."

"Really? You like them?"

"I love them. Or you could do your BLTs – the best this side of New York."

"But Sophie will be expecting something fancy."

"No, she won't. She gets gourmet food in Paris. Give her BLTs." He presses his mouth on mine and whispers through his kiss, "You're my Star-Spangled girl, remember? I don't care if you don't cook flashy, haute cuisine. I love you just the way you are. Don't ever change."

Sophie and Elodie arrive at eight o'clock sharp. Needless to say, every second has been spent by me preparing for their dreaded arrival. Patricia helped me lay the table with the best silver and crystal champagne glasses – BLTs in style with match-stick French fries and Bollinger Champagne. Because I'm the only native English speaker, the language du jour is soon French. Sophie has ways of looking as if she's the most charming person in the world while quietly stabbing me simultaneously. Alexandre doesn't seem to notice and Elodie is so busy stuffing her face with the BLTs, that she is blissfully unaware.

"So Pearl," Sophie begins. "How is everything going in zee Enterprise's department?"

"Great," I reply sweetly.

"She's just made a deal with Samuel Myers," Alexandre

interjects proudly. "He's a tough nut to crack and Pearl got what she wanted, namely a woman for one of the leads in *Stone Trooper.*"

Sophie smoothes her manicured hand over her sleek, chignon. "No! You're kidding me? Very talented actress, Alessandra Demarr."

The way she says that makes me wonder if she knew about this already. Although I do remember telling her I wanted women for the lead roles I don't remember anyone mentioning Alessandra Demarr. I wish Alexandre hadn't let her in on my business but answer simply, "Yes, I'm very pleased with the way things are going."

"I'm sure you'll be even more delighted as sings unravel zemselves to you," she says ominously - although the ominous vibe could just be my imagination. She's French – the translation may have come out wrong – 'things *unravel* themselves' – *what things?*

Alexandre puts his hand on mine. "Pearl's going to do some re-writing of the script, aren't you, darling? She always wanted to be a script writer and now's her chance."

Sophie's hand envelops both of ours, her eagle talons cupping us, her nails long and sharp. "Let's have a look at your engagement ring. Beeeootiful," she coos, gawking at it, her eyes wide.

"Thank you."

Alexandre looks pleased. "It belonged to a Russian princess, a lady in waiting, so to speak, to Catherine the Great."

Sophie cackles. "Cazerine zee Great - isn't she zee Empress who used to fuck horses?"

Elodie almost chokes on her champagne. "Maman!"

"No, seriously, rumor has it zat zay had to lower zee horse on top of her as no man's penis was big enough nor insatiable enough for her. Zay said she was a 'beastite' – I think zat's zee correct term. She died, in fact, trying to have sexual intercourse wiz a horse – she got crushed to death in zee act."

Alexandre bursts out laughing. "Nonsense. That was a myth, gossip spread by French aristocracy and her Polish enemies at the time to belittle her."

"Well, she certainly had a voracious sexual appetite which contributed to her downfall." Sophie turns to me and stares, her last sentence directed at me, for sure. I think of the Freudian dream I had about a black horse at the hotel in Cap d'Antibes, after Alexandre had been talking about getting me to 'ride' him. *Can Sophie read my frigging dreams?* She knows that I can't keep my hands off her brother. She knows my sexual appetite has been awakened. I look down at my empty glass awkwardly. Alexandre doesn't seem to notice what she has said and Elodie looks hazily at the *Tromp l'Oeil* of the dining room, settling her gaze onto the painted lake with swans and the fake view beyond that looks so disconcertingly real, obviously choosing not to follow the conversation.

"Well, I *love* your ring, Pearl," Sophie continues with a syrupy smile. "But why didn't you want a new piece of jewelry?"

"Pearl and I didn't want a blood diamond," Alexandre breaks in.

"A blood diamond?"

"A conflict diamond," I clarify. "A war diamond. A lot of top-grade diamonds are mined in war zones, particularly Africa. We didn't want to contribute to that in any way so Alexandre chose a vintage piece instead, and I'm glad he did."

Elodie pipes up, her pretty eyes wide, her interest piqued. "It's true, Natalie Portman does not wear real diamonds to Oscars or red carpet – she wears fake knock offs for five bucks for same reason."

I'm marveling at Elodie's colloquial English, using words like 'knock-offs' and 'bucks', and add, "It used to be a pendant and Alexandre had it made into a ring."

Sophie lets me know in a soft voice, "Well, I don't sink wearing someone's old jewelry is so lucky – bad Feng Shui, you know, could be bad vibe."

For the first time Alexandre looks angry. His mouth tenses as he says quietly between his teeth, "Actually, Sophie, I had the ring cleansed by a priest. By two different priests, in fact. Blessed with holy water. The ring is as pure as snow."

I look down at my achingly beautiful ring and wish Sophie hadn't laid her hands on it. As if her touch could pollute it in some way.

Swallowing a mouthful and then smiling sweetly she says, "These BLTs are so delicious, Pearl, you must tell me zee recipe."

Recipe. The recipe is in the *title of the sandwich*. BLT - bacon, lettuce and tomato. Of course, Sophie's irony is not lost on me but does seem to go over Alexandre's head. Men are so clueless when it comes to women's sharp claws disguised in white kid gloves. I tell Sophie, "The secret is in the bacon itself, Sophie. It's from a small farm Upstate where the pigs roam free in fields and lead a happy life."

Alexandre gets up from the table to get another bottle of champagne and Sophie whispers to me out of his earshot:

"Pearl, make sure you don't wear zat pearl choker my bruzzer gave you on your wedding day, itself. Pearls are unlucky for a bride, you know." Then she adds in a hoarse whisper, "I hope zat doesn't make *you* unlucky, having Pearl as your name."

I couldn't even remember how we got there. I guess it was by his car – what *was* his name? Later, I blanked that name out. Later, when it was all too…

Late.

My friend, Julia, had somehow slipped out of the equation. I was left with both boys, lascivious, like hungry dogs drooling for their dinner. But I was lapping up the attention, thinking of Brad studying with his new *girlfriend* – well I, too, could have some fun – two guys at once. An erotically-charged night – a threesome. A one-time pleasure adventure - just the once. Isn't that every girl's secret fantasy?

"Baby, what's wrong?"

My breath is short, my back is drenched with sweat. My eyes fly open and Alexandre is there beside me in bed. I heave a sigh of relief.

"You were having a bad dream, Pearl." He holds me close to him and kisses the lids of my wet eyes. "It's okay, everything's okay, baby. You can go back to sleep."

Alexandre brings me breakfast in bed the next morning. He sets down the tray and pours me coffee, adding steaming hot milk – a change from just the usual black caffeine fix that I always drink at work – he thinks the calcium is good for me. He knows just how I like it and it's always more delicious when he makes it than when I do it for myself. In every way he is the most sensitive man to my needs and desires, except in one aspect:

Sophie.

She is like the cliché Italian mother-in-law who wants to protect her son from the wicked influence of his wife or girlfriend. He is the eternal baby. Forever suspicious, she will always be jealous, no matter what you do or how you prove yourself. Sophie may be just his *sister* but because these siblings are so embroiled in HookedUp together this is a tough battle. She's a sister who is unfortunately embedded in my life, whether I like it or not. I am doing all I can not to nag. I have to be smart about this. My long game plan is to get her out of our lives.

"Alexandre," I begin, wondering how to broach the subject. "No, never mind."

"You want to tell me about these bad dreams you've been having, my darling?" he asks, sitting beside me on the bed. He's already dressed, ready for work.

I look at my watch and see I overslept. That dream has turned me upside down. "Actually," I venture, "I wanted to ask you if you noticed how…how spiky Sophie was being yesterday evening. I mean, she covered it up well with smiles but her intention was to make me look small."

He holds my hand. "Yes, I did notice. But the best thing to do with Sophie is ignore her when she's being like that. She wants to get a rise out of you – if you react it'll just feed her desire to overrun you even more. It's her way of getting your attention. Be flattered she's investing so much of her energy in you."

"*Flattered?* I'd like you to stop her behaving that way."

Alexandre shakes his head. "I can't stop her."

"Alexandre, why do you weaken when it comes to Sophie? If she's going to be like that, I don't want to see her. Period."

"Look, Sophie loves you."

"What?" I say incredulous. "Are you serious? She hates everything about me!"

"She was saying only yesterday how good you are for me. Singing your praises. That you're beautiful and have the face of an angel. She thinks your eyes are…what was the word she used? Yes, that's right…'soulful'. She loves you, Pearl. Believe me, if Sophie didn't like you, you'd soon realize. It's just her manner. Plus, her English comes out a bit strange sometimes…the translation goes a bit awry and things sound critical or odd but she doesn't mean it that way."

"She's playing us both, Alexandre." I sigh, exasperated. We are going nowhere with this conversation. "I wish I'd never agreed to the wedding gown gift."

But he just kisses me on the forehead as if I'm his little daughter who hasn't had her rest and is cranky from lack of sleep. "She adores you, Pearl. Now, I've got meetings all day so I'll see you later this evening. I'm taking you to the opera tonight."

"Wonderful," I mumble grumpily but then realize how spoiled that sounds so I ask with more energy, "What are we going to see?"

"Surprise."

I walk to work with Rex and decide to spend the day with Natalie. For some reason, I thought that working on feature films would be more exciting but I'm finding that I miss the detail of documentaries. There is something satisfying about delving into a world you would never normally encounter and unveiling truths and horrors that the normal public would never find out about. Sharing real life stories rather than selling fantasies – that is fulfilling.

Natalie's latest venture is into the dark cavern of modern slavery and human trafficking. This is something she feels passionate about as her ancestors were African slaves shipped to America. She's horrified that with all our education, this travesty is still happening all over the globe; the difference being that it is undercover and illegal, but nevertheless rife. I agree with her and think this project is crucial.

I find her in the editing room. The light is low and I study her concentrated hazel eyes set amidst her smooth café au lait-toned face. She is staring at the screen in the semi-darkness.

She clicks her fingers. "Cut right there," she instructs her assistant, John. "And then pick it up again at the voodoo dance bit." She looks at me out of the corner of her eye, "Hi, Pearl. We have so much footage I don't know how to squeeze it all in, in under just one hour."

"Make it ninety minutes, then."

"Can we get away with that?"

"Why not? I think people will be riveted by this story. We can do a special on it. I mean, this is world news. Most people think slavery finished with Abraham Lincoln – they need to know what's going on right here in New York City. Also, in London and Rome and in so many of the 'civilized' cities of the Western world."

Natalie wipes a tear from her cheek. "It breaks my heart."

Just as she says those words, Rex comes wagging up to her.

I laugh at his adorable dolphin face. Dogs can smile. "Mention the word 'heart'," I tell her, "and Rex will be at your side. He has an uncanny instinct when it comes to emotions. He can feel it when people are sad."

Natalie holds Rex's wide head in both hands and kisses him. "You sweet boy, just what the doctor ordered."

"By the way, sorry to change the subject but while it's on my mind, Dad called."

Natalie raises an eyebrow. "Did he now."

"He misses you and wonders why you won't return his calls."

"Men," she sighs.

"I think he loves you, Natalie."

"*Think* being the operative word."

"No, really, I'm sure of it. Every time Dad and I speak he wants to talk about *you*."

"Look, your dad is gorgeous. Very sexy, very attractive but as a human being he has a lot of failings. A lot. One of them being that he clams shut when it comes to his emotions. I'm sorry, Pearl, but I need a man who is more demonstrative."

"Well, I'm just passing this information on. Feel free to consider giving him another chance. You know, he is just a *guy*."

We laugh simultaneously.

"What about co-living with Alexandre? Any better with psycho sis?"

I tell her about my Zang Toi visit, my wedding gown and Sophie's snarky comments about my ring.

Natalie responds, "Clever woman. She has you over a barrel.

Buying you with an amazing gown – now she feels she has control over you."

"You make it sound as if I had a choice in the matter."

"We always have a choice, Pearl."

"I wish I could be more assertive like you, Natalie. You think I should cancel the gown, then?"

"It's a little late for that now. But don't have her over to your home anymore. Meet her at a restaurant, if need be – keep her at arm's length."

"I can assure you, there's no 'need be' – I'd be delighted if I never set eyes on her again."

We both fix our gaze on John for a moment as he prepares to show us more footage, and then Natalie says, "So pleased about Alessandra Demarr and that you came out on top getting a female lead."

"Girl power," I joke.

"You may laugh but it's true – we women need to look out for each other. When are you going to meet her?"

"It looks like Alexandre and I are going to Los Angeles in a few days. He's just waiting to hear back on something."

"Well, watch out for her."

"What do you mean?"

"She has a reputation, Pearl. She's a seductress."

"I have confidence in Alexandre – I trust him."

Natalie chuckles. "Not him, dummy. You. Be careful you don't fall for her charms."

The opera was awe-inspiring. A new soprano (whose name I can't pronounce) has everyone enthralled with her angelic voice. Afterwards, Alexandre and I went for a late supper and came home well after midnight.

I'm lying in bed unable to sleep. Not even sex has been able to calm my nerves; in fact, it made things worse. Natalie's film has been playing over and over in my mind. All I can think about is how men control so many parts of the world and women are their victims. Poor innocent girls, some as young as thirteen are being sold by their husbands or families in Nigeria – lured away for a 'better life' in Europe or The States, being promised lucrative jobs or an education but ending up working for the sex industry. An 'industry' it is with no thought for their feelings or their well being - like cattle they are being herded in droves.

How can there be so many monsters in this world? The image of Sula, one of the children in the film who was later lucky enough to have been saved, is turning over in my thoughts. Her large, doe-like eyes, her long, elegant neck; a sweet child who was abused by hundreds of men out for a cheap thrill. Cheap. As if she were worthless; just two holes - orifices for them to abuse. It makes me sick.

Finally, I drift off to a worrying sleep....

I lay down on the futon in just my bra and panties. The room was dimly lit with just a flickering candle. I felt nervous but excited. This was a first. I could hear them mumbling between themselves, discussing me. It was exhilarating to be the center of attention. I lay back, the tequila whooshing through my veins. I told them my name was Jane. Jane Doe. They were from another college, I'd probably never see them again but still, I didn't want to get a bad reputation – didn't want to be gossiped about. This was going to be a one-off, a secret. I wouldn't even tell Julia.

Jane Doe. I smiled to myself – I wondered if these boys believed my silly fib.

A firm hand touched my ankle, stroking me gently. Then a different hand, a little rougher, on my other calf. "Fuck, she's got a body on her," one said.

I looked at them hazily and saw the blonde one had his shirt off. He, too, had a body on him. He was a football player. They both were. I was in for a treat, I thought. My boyfriend Brad's body was different from these two – he was lithe and slim. He hated sports – he was too intellectual for that. These guys were hot. Dumb, from the basic way they spoke and the things they'd been saying all evening like, 'stoked' and 'dude' - their vocabulary was limited, but they were hot, nevertheless.

One hand trailed up my leg and lingered on my thigh. I felt myself clench inside and I gasped.

"Turn over," the blonde one said.

I turned on my stomach. He unclasped my bra and I felt some warm oil being rubbed on my back. Four hands were massaging me and it felt incredible, the knots in my shoulders being kneaded away. One set of hands was working on my upper body and the other traced down to my ass, cupping it, squeezing it; the fingers brushing past my crack. I moaned. This felt amazing. The same hand parted the cleft in my butt and trailed an index finger along it, resting at my entrance. I could sense my moistness gather, my clit tingling with pleasure. The hands moved down my thighs, and then up again, I could feel a hand press against my panties and his finger exploring my opening.

"She's as wet as a wetback, dude," one said and they both laughed.

Blood rushed to my head for a second, riled by the racist comment - normally something I would have jumped at - but I felt so good, so relaxed, the liquor coursing through my body, throbbing in my groin.

The other pair of hands moved underneath me, caressing my belly, then cupping my whole mound, the base of his palm pushing in just the perfect spot. I groaned and took his hand, thrusting it against my clit and I lifted my stomach upwards off the futon and pressed hard back down on it again. I felt so aroused.

"Jesus, her pussy's wet," this one said. He opened my legs apart and slipped his fingers inside me with one hand and peeling my panties off with the other.

"Turn back over," the other one said. "I want to suck those hot tits." He pushed my body so it rolled like a heavy stone. He pulled off my bra. I felt woozy. I was now on my back, my eyes closed. I could smell some patchouli incense coiling in the air, rich and thick. My head was propped up by cushions.

The blonde one edged further down the bed and prized my thighs apart with his hands. "Gotta chow down on this pussy," he told me with a sexy groan. His tongue darted out at my clit and I could feel my body, almost as if it didn't belong to me, writhing with desire. He pressed his entire mouth over my folds and began to lash his tongue up and down my cleft then circle my clit with his flipping tongue. I arched my back up high and moaned, pressing myself against his mouth.

The other guy was sucking my nipples. Nibbling on them, gently tugging with his teeth. "Christ, this feels incredible," I whimpered, the alcohol drumming through my veins.

I flexed my hips even closer to the blonde one's mouth. I

could feel the need building, the need to be penetrated as the guy working on my torso flicking his tongue again on my hard nipple making it pucker. He then kneeled up and I saw his erection press towards my face.

"Suck my dick," he commanded.

I could feel the other guy's finger slide inside me. "Gotta fuck this pussy," he said.

The other one shoved his penis in my face. I held my breath – the reality of what I had got myself into suddenly hit me.

I heard him say to his friend, "Wait up, dude, she's gotta suck my dick first. I wanna come inside her mouth. I want her to lick her sweet tongue all over my cock and suck it till my hot, creamy cum jets out to the back of her throat. Then I'm gonna fuck her, fuck that tight, horny little cunt – fuck it till she's begging me to stop."

"Dude, *I've* gotta bone her first – she's got my dick so pumping and hard – gotta fuck that wet cunt – gonna make that cunt come all over my cement-hard dick."

I need air. I need space.

"Wake up!"

I don't want to open my eyes. I don't want to see.

"Darling, wake up!"

I dare to peel open my eyes and see Alexandre's concerned face staring at me. I let out the breath I've been holding in – my lungs expire with relief.

Alexandre shakes his head. "There's something wrong. I don't understand. Why all of a sudden these nightmares? Baby, what's wrong?" He grips me tight and covers my face with kisses.

"Just a bad dream."

"You were moaning – muttering in your sleep. Everything

seemed fine at first, your lips were even curved in a smile but then you started thrashing about the bed and crying out. Tell me about your dream, Pearl, baby. Maybe if you speak about it, these nightmares will go away.

"I can't remember," I lie. "I don't remember. Please just hold me, Alexandre."

6

Los Angeles has not let us down. The sky is so blue that just looking at it makes you feel warm and happy, as if you've never had a problem in your life. The palm trees line Sunset Boulevard, the leaves shimmering in a gentle breeze as we cruise along in our rented 1960's Cadillac convertible. It's powder blue. Only in LA.

I remember that when I lived here, brief as it was, I felt that I was on vacation every single day, even though I had a nine to five job. People are easy in Los Angeles and constantly in a good mood. They don't call it La La Land for nothing. Beneath the veneer of perfection lie secrets and a dark interior but why delve deep when you can savor the trappings of glitz? At least for a little while.

Sunset Boulevard is a winding road, over twenty miles long linking the urban streets of downtown to the grand and glamorous residential avenues of Beverly Hills, Bel-Air and

Brentwood. It continues to the Pacific Coast Highway in Malibu, passing some of the most beautiful properties that money can buy. Why take the freeway when you can soak up the ambience of the old-style Hollywood allure along this stretch? Gloria Swanson immortalized this place with her 1950's film, *Sunset Boulevard* – I imagine the debauched parties that were held in the exquisite homes here, the deals, the passion and the back-stabbing divorces that followed.

Alexandre's left elbow rests languidly on the sill of the open window, a content smile on his handsome face as the wind laps his dark hair – neither of us speaking, just enjoying the music; a golden oldie, *Hotel California*.

We're headed to Alessandra Demarr's house in Topanga Canyon, an interesting choice for an abode, once famous for being an artists' colony. She has invited us for lunch. I don't know why but I'm feeling nervous.

We arrive at our destination although it's not quite as elegant as I had imagined. Our low automobile has trouble on the bumpy, pot-holed driveway which crosses a creek where frogs are croaking – not your typical Hollywood mansion. Who is this woman? Everybody has been raving about her acting abilities and her brooding beauty. I'm already intimidated by her.

Alexandre parks the car in an opening where the driveway seems to come to an abrupt end. There are no houses about, or at least, none that I can see.

"Did we make a wrong turn?" I ask him.

"This is where the GPS directed us," he answers looking about. There are some lemon trees and rolling, scrubby hills in the distance and exposed bedrock. I even see a vegetable plot and beyond it a sort of shack. There's a black vintage Porsche, dusty from passing along this makeshift driveway, no doubt, parked in a corner.

Just then, a figure appears from behind a hedge. A sunbeam of light catches her and she's wearing a long, black dress. She's slim and when she walks she glides as if she were not part of this world. For a second, I think I must have seen a ghost. But it must be Alessandra Demarr.

She grins at us and calls over, "You made it! Shows you must be in the top four percent of the intelligent population – you'd be amazed how this place has most people flummoxed." Her accent is vaguely Italian but obviously she has mastered the English language with a word like flummoxed. I look at Alexandre to see if he's as bowled over as I am by her beauty but he seems nonchalant as if seeing stunning women is part of his daily routine. He walks over to greet her and she immediately offers both cheeks.

I do the same. When I kiss her, her skin is soft as down and she smells delicious, of flowers and sweetness; femininity seeping from every pore. I step back and my breath hitches. Her thick, wavy hair is almost wild, like a teenager who hasn't brushed it in days. The dark locks hang down her bronzed back, her shoulders are strong but slight, her breasts pert but not large - you can see straight away that she isn't wearing a bra. Again, my eyes flit over to Alexandre to gauge his expression but he seems unimpressed by her. Her teeth are flaming white and her smile stretches across her face – a Julia Roberts sort of smile, warm and friendly.

"You know what? I'm starving," she cries, "as I skipped breakfast. D'you mind if we eat something straight away? I've prepared some antipasti to nibble on. Then I have a home-baked pizza cooking away in my wood-fired pizza oven."

I lick my lips. "Wow, you have a special pizza oven?"

"Made by hand by an Italian guy who lives nearby."

"Count me in!" I say.

"Where are you guys staying?" she asks.

"In Santa Monica," Alexandre tells her, edging towards the old Porsche. Is this car yours? It's a 356B, isn't it? Let me guess, 1962?"

"Yes, you're right. Poor thing, she needs a wash," Alessandra says with a laugh, and then links her arm in mine and pulls me towards the gap in the hedge from where she emerged five minutes ago like a dark angel. "Boys - always obsessed by bits of metal. Sniff about her, Alexandre, why don't you. Take her for a spin if you like – the keys are under the matt. Meanwhile, I'm going to feed your fiancée some snacks and give her a Bloody Mary. Come join us when you've finished with your testosterone boost. Anyway, I want to have your beautiful Pearl all for myself for a while and talk shop. Go for a drive, Alexandre - take my car along the coast."

Alexandre laughs out loud. "I can see you're desperate to get rid of me."

"Just for a little," she says, tossing her dark mane. "Come back in half an hour." She pulls me close and walks me away from him. I look behind and he winks at me in amusement, settling himself in the driver's seat of her classic car.

"See you in a bit," he calls out but Alessandra ignores him and rakes her gaze over me from my head to my toes. I'm wearing just a dress and some flat Greek sandals. A frisson of nervousness shoots through my body. No woman has ever looked at me this way before.

Once through the secret entrance in the hedge, I set my eyes on her house; a glorified barn made of wooden clapperboard and with a garden surrounding it of roses and more lemon trees. There's a little tree house looking like something out of *Robinson Crusoe* and a hammock resting between two small oaks. Beyond, I see a swimming pool, the water shimmering and breaking up into fragments of wavy light from dark blue mosaic tiles. The place is magical and from another world. The antithesis of 'Hollywood' or how you imagine it should be.

"He's cute your husband-to-be," she notes. "Very sexy French yet with a body like an American movie star – before and during filming, you know, when they're in perfect shape." She throws her head back and laughs. "He's very Alpha male. I bet he's a great fuck."

My mouth hangs open at what she just said. I'm speechless. I've known her for less than ten minutes. I reply simply, "Yes, he is."

"Of course, that's something I don't do anymore, but sometimes I miss that, you know, I miss that hard rod between my legs. But the whole man thing is such a bore. The pride, the bullshit and they just don't *smell* like we do. There's nothing like a woman's touch to make you feel like you've come home."

At the words 'woman's touch' she places her hand on the small of my back, letting her fingertips linger on my butt. I think of Natalie's warning and know that this woman is just beginning. I feel scared but thrilled and mostly, curious. Not even Alexandre came on so strong when he met me. Then it suddenly hits me. The names:

Alexandre.

Alessandra.

The yin and the yang.

Why is this woman making me feel as if I have no control? As if she's running the show? What happened to Pearl the ball-buster? Is it because Alessandra has no balls *at all* that I am at a loss for words?

I wriggle away from her contact but she grabs my hand instead and leads me to the pool.

"I'm hot," she says, and pulls her slinky dress over her head. She isn't wearing anything underneath. I glance awkwardly at her body. It's perfect. Her legs are smooth and long, her golden arms hang cool beside her hips. Her breasts are perfect and not surgically enhanced like so many actresses here, but curve upwards like full but perky teardrops, the nipples pert and small. She catches me watching her and smiles seductively, the dimple on one cheek reminds me eerily of Alexandre when he looks at me that way. It's uncanny. She's like a female version of him. He may be Alpha male but she's an Alpha female, all woman. Tough but whimsical, strong but softly feminine. Her eyes are also green like his but more feline. The similarities between them are frightening.

"Come in, the water's perfect," she entreats after she has accomplished a perfect swallow dive. Her hair is now sleek on her head and her eyes dark from run mascara – it makes her the epitome of a Hollywood 'femme fatale'.

I take off my sandals and dip my toes in the water. It really is warm and I'm tempted.

"Come on, don't be shy. Nobody's allowed in this pool with a swimsuit – only skinny-dipping here at all times. Come in, Pearl."

I slip my dress over my shoulders and stand there in my bra and panties. A matching, pale pink lace set from La Perla that Alexandre surprised me with the other day. I suddenly feel awkward and embarrassed – *I don't know this woman!* "You know what? I think I'll just dangle my feet in and wait until Alexandre gets back."

Her eyes narrow. "I won't bite, you know," and then she dives down and does a handstand, her elegant toes as pointed as a ballerina. She emerges from the water and looks like a Bond girl, all sex, heat, and temptress. As if she were designed by God to do nothing but seduce. I turn my eyes away and reach for my dress and struggle back into it – I should never have taken it off in the first place.

"Come, I'm going to make you the best Bloody Mary you've ever tasted," she tells me, water dripping off her tanned body as she grabs a towel.

I follow her to the kitchen which is country-style with a large pine table in the middle and baskets of dried flowers hanging from rafters and wooden beams. She takes a jug out of the refrigerator and pours the mixture into two tall glasses, garnishing them with sticks of celery and lemon slices. She hands me a glass. "Here, try this, it has a kick to it, a touch of horseradish. And help yourself to my spread of cold meats and *bruschetta*. The basil's fresh from the garden and the tomatoes from my greenhouse. Oh, and the olive oil I brought from Sicily where my grandparents are from. It has a nutty taste – quite delicious. Actually, let's take it all outside on the porch."

We put everything on a tray and take it outside where there's a wrought iron table and chairs. I delve into the *bruschetta* and can taste the sun in the tomatoes. It's true, the olive oil is sublime.

"So Pearl, Sam says we need to get to work on the script straight away."

"We?"

"You didn't think you'd be doing it all alone, did you? No, no, my darling, this needs to be team work. I want the script to feel natural to me. You know, be part of who I am."

But you're an actress, ACT! "Oh, Sam made out that I'd be working with just the script writer, he never mentioned that you wanted to be involved," I say as politely as I can.

"Nuh, uh, I want to put in my twopence worth - I want to have my say."

"With all due respect, Alessandra, that wasn't part of the deal - it wasn't written into your contract."

She pouts her lips like a child. "But Sam wants me to be happy. Don't you?"

I take a sip of my Bloody Mary and then reply, "Well of course I do. I think an actor's input is very important but you know, too many cooks can spoil the broth."

"I just need a week with you. Just so you get to know me. I thought we could do a little improvisation, you know, have some fun."

"But we're only here for three days and then we have to get back to New York."

"Who has to get back to New York?" It's Alexandre. He comes up behind me and massages my shoulders. His touch is warm. I feel a wave of relief wash over me.

"Hi Frenchie," she says. "Hope you had fun with my car. Just trying to persuade your other half to stay on a few days. You know, we need to work on the script together before the others get hold of it. I want it to be our baby."

Alexandre laughs. I can see her flirtatiousness toward me is amusing him for some reason. Even calling him *Frenchie*. I feel as if I'm being fed to the wolves when he says to me, "Stay, darling.

Enjoy this beautiful LA weather - relax a little. I can't as I've got a meeting in Montreal but there's no reason why you shouldn't."

"No way," I state assertively. "I have to get back to Manhattan. Natalie and I are working on something very important. She needs me in the editing room."

"Nonsense. That was your old job, remember? You're on features now, not documentaries. Natalie can take care of it all herself,"

Whose side are you on? But all I say is, "I'll call Sam later and discuss it with him."

Just then a black cat shimmies its way around my bare legs. Its soft fur seductive, its purr intense.

"That's Lucifer," Alessandra tells me. "He's an Oriental. Isn't he the most handsome thing you've ever set your eyes on?"

The cat continues to purr and rub itself against me. Why do I have this ominous feeling that between Lucifer and Alessandra I don't stand a chance?

On the way back to the hotel Sam calls and confirms my worries. He wants Alessandra to 'assist' me with script changes. He tells me that the buzz is out and he wants this film to not only be a blockbuster but 'a classy blockbuster' - to have a chance to be nominated for an Academy Award. He feels that Alessandra is going to put it into a higher category because she's a 'real actress' and that we need to respect her wishes. He persuades me that I need to stay on a few more days, work with her before handing our changes over to the main script doctor. It all feels odd but as

I am a virgin to the world of movie producing, I have to take his word for it.

Alexandre and I are sitting on the balcony of our luxurious room which overlooks the ocean. We're listening to the rhythmical sound of the surf and enjoying the feeling of being on vacation. I'm using this opportunity to discuss Sam and Alessandra with him and the rather bizarre situation.

Alexandre kisses my hand and says, "You make it sound as if it's some sort of punishment, Pearl – don't be so worried. How bad can it be to hang out in the sunshine with a beautiful actress while you fiddle about with the script?"

I sigh and fix my eyes on some surfers in the distance waiting to catch the next big wave. "She's just so persuasive, so...so..."

A mischievous smile spreads across his gorgeous face. "You're worried she's going to try and seduce you."

I look into his sparkling, amused eyes. "Yes."

"Ooh, how *dangerous*," he teases. *Don gaire oose*, his accent says.

"You're laughing about it now but what happens if she succeeds?"

"Sexy." He grins. "You can sex Skype me - the pair of you. I can't think of anything that would turn me on more. Two beautiful women getting it on together – two sexy female bodies entwined. Feel my cock," he says, taking my hand and putting it on his crotch, "I'm hard just thinking about you two together."

I rub his huge stiff erection through his jeans but I take my hand away and say, "Seriously, Alexandre, she means business, I can tell."

"Have some fun and come straight back home. I'm not worried, Pearl - not in the least."

"What, even if something were to actually happen? If she

kissed me or…or…something more?"

He laughs, then presses his lips lightly on my temple.

"You're acting like this whole thing is a joke," I blurt out, a touch annoyed. "You might get jealous if something really did *take place.*"

"Baby, she's a *woman*. How could I feel threatened by a woman?"

"What if a guy was coming on to me like this?"

Alexandre's smile fades and a flash of irritation dances in his green eyes. "That would be a whole different story. I wouldn't be allowing you to stay on in LA if some good-looking movie actor was demanding to co-write with you, I can tell you."

"But this is my *job*, you can't dictate to me who I work with!"

"I'm your fiancé. Didn't anyone ever warn you that Frenchmen have a possessive streak?"

I think of Daisy's wise advice: *He's a Latin man at heart.* "So you speak for the whole of France?" I ask with a laugh. "Or is it just a small minority of you who suffer from jealousy?"

"Not jealous, just claiming what belongs to me, that's all."

"Yet a woman couldn't possibly pose a threat? A woman isn't as powerful as a man, is that what you're saying?"

"Now you're twisting things. A woman doesn't have a penis."

I roll my eyes. "Ah, so it boils down to that, does it? The testosterone factor!"

"Maybe."

"So how would you feel about any of my past instances with men? How would you feel if you knew I'd been… promiscuous once upon a time?"

"Well, I happen to know that you weren't. You had a steady boyfriend, what was his name? Brad, that's right, the brother of your best friend…you dated him for four years and then you got married several years later. I don't see someone graduating summa cum laude and doing as well as you did academically, running around fucking lots of guys. Besides, it doesn't go with your personality."

"But let's just say, for argument's sake, that I *had* been running around, but it was−"

His cell rings and our conversation is over. It's his sister. Of course. As if she can hear what we're saying. Sometimes I wonder if she isn't sneaking recording bugs into the room to spy on us. Alexandre ends the call and now I feel compelled to speak out. This time, about Sophie.

"Alexandre - before we became engaged, you told me that you'd be opting out of HookedUp, that you and Sophie would go your separate ways."

"That's my plan. But all in good time, darling, all in good time. That's what HookedUp Enterprises is about − you and me. The two of us veering off in a new direction without Sophie."

I knit my brows. "When will 'good time' be?"

"As soon as the moment is right."

Getting nowhere with this, I return to Conversation One. "So to be completely clear, if something happened between me and Alessandra, hypothetically speaking, because I have no intention of letting her get her way, but if it did, you wouldn't consider that I was being unfaithful to you, or cheating on you in some way?"

"No, not all at."

"Just double-checking," I say.

Later, Alexandre goes surfing. He's dressed in a black, rubber, short-sleeved suit; his pecs defined and the bulge of his biceps accentuated by the outfit. I sit on the beach, a cardigan wrapped about me with my headphones on, listening to the perfect soundtrack by the Beach Boys, *Surfin' USA* as I watch my fiancé take each wave, moving his body in elegant swivels and jumps, flowing with the surf, bending and straightening his body at each perfect moment. He makes it look effortless, gliding with precision under each barreling wave, never flinching, never falling. He surfs as well as my father and that's really saying something. My stomach flips at his prowess – there's nothing like watching a man excel at sport.

I feel warm inside. I love this man more than ever.

7

It was pressed up against my face - I was gasping for air.

The boys' repeated use of the word 'cunt' was drumming in my ears. I hated that word – it was vulgar, demeaning to women - it made me feel cheap. I opened my eyes and saw the guy's long, skinny penis and his hand fumble again on my face. I could almost smell his hyped-up hormones - the whole scenario was suddenly grossly wrong – disconnected from the person I was inside. How did I get to this point? What happened? I felt sick at myself. I had only slept with Brad up until now. What had I been *thinking?*

Needle-dick pressed his thin, lanky erection on my mouth once more and shouted, "Suck my goddam dick, goddam it!"

I tried to maneuver myself up against the pillows but my head was spinning fast. The other guy was on top of me now and I could hardly breathe with his weight. "Guys," I said, "I don't want to do this. It was a bad idea. I'm drunk – I had too much tequila." I pushed my arms out at the blonde one's chest to get him off me but I couldn't even see past the other guy who was prizing open my lips with his clammy, smelly fingers trying to stuff his needle-like erection into my mouth. I gagged with repulsion.

"I'm going to be sick," I moaned, flailing my arms about and then tried to lever myself off the futon. "Please you two, I want to go home now...please somebody drive me home...I don't want to do this." My words were slurring but they understood. "Guys, I apologize for leading you on but I don't want to do this anymore. I made a big mistake, I just wanna go back to my dorm."

"Fuck you, bitch, suck my fucking dick!" He was pumping his hips into my face now, his hand grabbing my long hair like rope as his hot, sweaty balls were squashing against my closed lips.

"Get off!" I screamed, shaking my head and protecting my face with my hands. "Get the fuck off me, don't you *get* it, the party's OVER!"

"Get the fuck off her dude," the blonde one said pushing Needle-dick away from me.

Thank God, I thought, and I took a desperate lungful of air, so relieved his crotch was out of my face. But the blonde one then said, "I'll fuck her first and then you can have her after me."

"Fuck you, asshole, she was gonna suck me off!"

"She's wasted, dude, can't you see that? The slut's off her fuckin' face. It's really taking effect now. Let me have her first."

I started to scream and thrash about but the blonde one held my wrists together in a tight vice and the other one muffled my mouth with his stinky palm. The blond was powerful, his football-trained muscles rippling beneath his chest. As I tried to sit up in one great burst of effort my head started to spin and I saw stars trail about the room in waves. He crashed back on top of me and forced my legs open with his knees. I tried to free my hands to scratch him but I was still immovable. He started pumping into me, his elbow still holding down my arms. My legs were kicking in the air but my attempt to get him off me was pathetically weak. This guy was super-strong. The more I shouted and thrashed the more turned on he got.

"That's right, fuck that horny little slut, dude – you know she wants it," Needle-dick chanted, getting a vicarious thrill out of watching his friend pound me while he simultaneously played with himself.

The blond's breath was hoarse with whiskey as he panted his way to a fast orgasm. Jesus, I realized - he wasn't even wearing a condom. He pulled out immediately and rolled off me. I lurched up to stand but the other one grabbed my ankles in a rugby tackle and I went flying face-down on the futon, my head slapping hard against the pillows.

"Don't think you can run off, you cock-teasing slut! I haven't even started yet." He rolled me over and smashed on top of me, lustily pinning me down. He too was brawny, my inebriated body, now feeling almost numb, was no match for his big, clumping frame. I clasped my legs tightly together so he couldn't enter me but he wrenched my thighs open and poked his weapon inside. I bashed his back with my fists but it was like pummeling a brick wall. Grunting, he thumped himself further inside my vulnerable spot forcing my legs further open. I screamed but nobody seemed to hear. Where was everyone? By this point, I blanked out. I held my head to the side and closed my lips tight. Of all the horrors, being kissed seemed the most disgusting of all. If I could at least keep my mouth untainted, I'd be winning on some level. I felt repulsed at myself, horrified that I got my sorry ass into this mess but all I could concentrate on was survival and somehow getting out of there. I eyed my clothing strewn about the floor and planned my getaway. The second he was done, I'd grab my stuff and charge out of the door. My shoes I'd leave, I'd need to be barefoot to move fast.

But then I heard another voice; a new guy barging into the room. My heart leaped into my stomach with both hope and dread. Would he save me? Or were things about to get much worse?

My lungs are heaving, my chest tight - I feel suffocated. I open my eyes and hear the reassuring sound of the surf and feel a cool morning breeze wafting through the window. The sheets are crumpled in a mess. I've been kicking, tossing and turning. I hear the shower next door – thank God, Alexandre is in the bathroom - he hasn't been witness to yet another of my nightmares.

I get out of bed, holding my stomach. I feel nauseous and think I may throw up. I sit on one of the comfy chairs on our balcony and breathe in the fresh, salty air. I already feel better. All of my past is surging back – the buried memories which I thought had been blanked out of my life. No wonder men grossed me out for so many years. Holy shit!

Alexandre finds me on the balcony. He's dripping wet with a towel tied around his middle of his toned abs. I look at him, taking in his physical beauty and wonder if he would have once been capable of doing what those boys did. Are all men pigs at heart? Is it just a question of circumstance? Perhaps those guys are all happily married now with sweet, adoring children who look up to them and think that they're the best dads in the world.

Wives who would never believe you if you enlightened them to what their husbands had once done in their college years.

Nobody would blame them. Guys are guys. Girls should know better, shouldn't they? Women should be smarter, not put themselves in precarious situations, not 'ask for it'. Not behave like 'sluts'.

Alexandre comes over to me and gives me a hug. "You look very pensive, Pearl. What's on your mind?"

"Just looking at the beautiful view thinking how wonderful it would be to live by the ocean."

"Funny, I was thinking exactly the same thing. I feel a real estate goblin knocking at my door. Shall we buy something here?"

"I still can't get used to this," I murmur.

"What?"

"Buying whatever your heart desires. It makes me feel guilty somehow."

"Hey, I work hard for these privileges. You do, too."

"I know. Just…well, we're still so lucky."

He holds my hands and pulls me off the chair. "Come to bed for a little while. You look so sexy, Pearl – I love you in the morning all ruffled up. It makes me want to get as close to you as is physically possible."

His body is so beautiful, my heart yearns for him, but the truth is that sex is the last thing on my mind, even with the man I love more than anything in the world. I melt into his strong arms and nuzzle my face against his warm chest and lick off a few droplets of shower water. He smells of soap and his own natural Alexandre magic – he is my elixir, the potion I need to keep me healthy and sane. I kiss him all over with sweet, girlish kisses. I want to be loving, not sexy, but it makes him groan and I can feel his erection press up against me.

I peel away the towel around his waist and see his beautiful anatomy, a penis that is substantial but wonderful because it has never tried to hurt me or force me. Even that time that he was angry with me, after I hadn't been honest with him about who I was and he came barging into my apartment...even then when he took me in the kitchen and ravaged me right there and then...he knew I was desperate for him and if I had told him to stop he would have.

I bend down and kiss him below his waist and breathe him in - his kindness, his patience, his genuine love. And then I let out a sigh of relief; gratitude that he is the way he is. I look up at him like a puppy.

He strokes my hair. "Pearl, darling, what's with the tears?"

"Tears of love," I reply.

He takes me over to the bed. I feel a tingle in my groin and realize that I'm moist between the legs. He does that to me because I trust him with every fiber of my being. His finger glides between my slick folds and he slips it gently inside me, letting just a hint of pressure tantalize my clit. "You're so sexy, so wet. I need you baby, I need to be inside you. How I'm going to get through this week without making love to you, I don't know." His mouth is on mine, pressed hard over my lips and I respond with desire, meeting his tongue with little licks. He groans again and pushes me on the bed, his strong body covering me whole. I feel all-feminine underneath his strapping frame.

I open my legs and cling to his firm torso, my arms gripping around his muscular back and I claw my nails into him without meaning to. "Please fuck me," I beg, confused as to the double emotions I feel inside. I want to prove to myself that everything's okay. That no past ghosts can come between me and the man I love. "I need you and only you," I murmur.

He slips inside me, his mouth again on mine and he slowly pushes his way further between my cleft, his erection taut and full, stretching me open, his pubic bone pressing deliciously on my clit. He's staring into my eyes. He takes my clawed hands one by one away from his back and holds my wrists together above my head with just one hand. He is claiming me, dominating me - I can't escape from this position but it's okay because it's him. I feel the power of his extensive thick cock cramming me full, pumping into me. I push my hips higher to meet him and we thrust together in a natural rhythm, each time we meet all my nerves are tingling with need.

"Don't stop, I think I'm going to come – keep doing what you're doing," I moan.

"I'll never stop. Never."

I can feel it building, feel that glorious sensation of blood rushing up inside the core of me when he says, "I love being inside you, baby…fucking you…and you know what else?"

"Tell me," I plead. "Tell me what you love." I'm gyrating my hips now - I need to be as close as is humanly possible.

"I love kissing you, running my tongue along your sexy lips when I'm deep inside you." His mouth is on mine as he says this.

I'm thrusting hard, pressing my clit against him…this feels incredible. "Tell me what I can do to please you," I say with urgency. "Tell me what you love."

"When you suck my cock tightly with your pretty lips, when my cock is deep inside your hot mouth."

Suddenly, a vision of the needle-dick guy flashes through my mind. I catch my breath but not in a good way. I was on the brink of orgasm but not any more…I close my eyes to make the image go away and then open them again to drink in Alexandre, to reassure myself that he is different, that he has nothing to do with these repulsive snap-shots. I get back to my rhythm – I need this release - but more images come crashing through me…being forced, pushed, pulled, not being able to escape. Needle-dick again, suffocating my mouth. I feel panicked and smothered. Alexandre is pressing his body against me passionately and all I can think of are dirty, smelly cocks and rape and tequila and my body as weak and helpless as a rag doll….

"Alexandre, I can't…sorry, I feel sick…I think I'm going to barf….please…"

He freezes his position and releases my wrists but it's too late…I can feel his cock swelling and hot rush spurt deep inside me. He is instantly contrite and says, "I'm sorry, baby, I couldn't help myself; you're so fucking sexy the way you move. What's wrong, chérie?" Slowly, he pulls out. He rolls off me to give me the space I crave.

I lie there hyperventilating.

"Are you okay, baby?" He looks shocked with concern, puts his hand in mine and kisses my fingertips softly. He pulls me off the bed and ushers me to the bathroom. I stand there with my face in my hands, my head bent down. I turn on the shower faucet. I need to get clean. I need to wash this morning's dream away. I feel the sticky mess of Alexandre's cum trickling down my inner thighs and even though it emanates from pure love and goodness, from a man who would lay his life down for me, I feel sickened.

Penises. Cocks. Dicks. Blowjobs. Semen.

I am disgusted.

I'm hoping this feeling will fade but as the day draws on it gets worse – the straw that breaks the camel's back is a video clip Natalie sends me of her documentary about child trafficking for the insatiable sex industry. Men are pigs whichever way you look at it. Aided, sadly, by women sometimes, even by mothers selling their own daughters - but still, who is fucking these young girls (and sometimes boys) - women? No, men are the devils with their penises ruling their brains. Not women but *men*.

Poor Alexandre is the innocent victim of my sudden repulsion towards all things male, although when I look into his beautiful eyes I don't feel anything but love and compassion for him. My heart aches – he is my everything. None of this is his fault.

But the idea of being penetrated, right now, revolts me. Please God, let this feeling go away. I love sex with him so much…

Luckily, he's flying out late tonight so I won't have to explain myself. On two occasions this afternoon, my whole story nearly escaped my lips but something held me back. Why subject him to my baggage? Give it a few days – let the memory ride itself out and I'll be back to normal. At least the dreams are unleashing it all, revealing the truth of what really happened that night – things my conscious mind had blocked out.

It wasn't my fault as I had always led myself to believe. Or was it? If I tell Alexandre I'd have to explain to him how I got myself into that predicament in the first place. A threesome with two footballers? His vision of me as the perfect summa cum laude student with the unblemished past would be shattered. No - let his perception of me remain untainted, at least until I feel confident enough to reveal everything. Remembering all this is bad enough, but if he finds it hard to accept? If he has it lurking in the back of his mind every time we have sex, then what?

I need time. I need a few days to think this all through.

We spend the day walking along the beach and then pass by Venice to see the wild and wonderful attractions. There's a hippie guitar player zipping along on roller-skates and a bottle-blond Tarzan character working out in an outdoor gym with massive weights, right by the Boardwalk for everyone to see. There are volleyball and paddle tennis courts and funky shops, cafés and vendor booths lined along this long stretch on Ocean Front Walk. We meander, people-watching, taking in the sights of colorful street performers and beautiful young things strutting their stuff in skimpy outfits – Venice Beach is an exhibitionist haven.

The distractions are perfect; enough for Alexandre to not realize that anything is particularly wrong. When he asked me earlier what happened in bed this morning and I told him that it must have been the smoothie I drank the day before - a mild case of food poisoning - he believed me.

And like food poisoning I *will* kick this out of my system. I will. It is in the *past*, something that happened so long ago it has no business screwing up my life now. I won't let it dominate my thoughts; I won't let it make me bitter and angry. I was a different person then, anyway – I made a foolish decision, and I paid a price for it. Does that mean it has to affect my life now?

That I have to keep paying that price? Affect the person I am today?

As Alexandre and I continue our walk - arm in arm, I notice people looking at my fiancé, eyeballing him up and down with come-on stares and I feel proud. Yes, he's handsome, girls and boys, and you know what? He's *mine*.

Perhaps the break of a few days will be good for us. I can sort my scrabbled head out. I'll call Daisy and talk it through with her – maybe even see a therapist here.

I crook my arm tighter with his. "I'll miss you."

He winks at me. "It's only five more days. You'll be so busy you won't even notice."

"And you? What will you be doing?"

"Making money for us to get a pad here."

"A pad?"

"Something wonderful. Further up the coast in Malibu. A house overlooking the water where I can surf and you can walk along the beach with Rex and swim if you're brave enough to brace the cold – would you like that?"

"No, it would make me miserable. Too much of a punishment."

He laughs and pulls me closer. "You don't have to go to work, you know."

"What d'you mean?" I ask, confused.

"You don't have to prove yourself to me. I know you're clever at your job but if you feel like packing it all in and do nothing but read novels and lie about in the sun, I wouldn't think any less of you."

I grin. "I don't know how long I'd last doing that. Sounds tempting, though. But I've always worked. Even at school I had a

Saturday job – I don't know if lazing about is my style."

"Well, just letting you know that you have a get-out clause. Just because we started HookedUp Enterprises doesn't mean you have to be chained to it for forever."

"What about you? You wouldn't ever have to work another day in your life if you didn't want to, either, but you keep going with all these endless meetings all over the place."

"Just say the word, baby, and we can go and live in a tree-house in Thailand. Or join your father in Kauai."

"You mean that?"

"I think so. Although, the truth is, I've always worked, too. I had jobs from the age of nine."

"But that's illegal in France, isn't it? Children working?"

"Nothing about my life was legal when Sophie was playing mother to me after we left home – after we left that monster," he spits out between his teeth, his mouth bitterly tight.

"Your mother must feel so guilty about not having come with you when she had the chance."

"She does. Her guilt is almost tangible. Every time I see her, her eyes spell out regret."

"You know that Edith Piaff song?"

"Why is it, Pearl, that you and I can read each other's minds? I was just thinking the same thing! *Non, je ne regrette rien…*"

He starts singing. He has a good voice, perfectly in tune.

"*Do* you regret anything, Alexandre?"

He squeezes my hand. "I regret not having kissed you sooner."

"No, seriously, if you could re-live your life what would you choose to do differently?"

"I am who I am because of all my choices, the good and the

bad. Perhaps if I'd done everything in the perfect order I'd be married to Laura, and you and I would have never met."

"D'you still think about her?"

"She's a dear friend, we shared a past, of course I still care for her and worry about her wellbeing."

A clown comes bounding in front of us, interrupting our heart-to-heart conversation. *Not Now!* I glare at him and his painted face and turn my head back to Alexandre, "So you don't agonize over choices you made in the past or about things you wish you hadn't done?"

"Sometimes you don't have a choice, Pearl. Sometimes external forces choose for you."

"Natalie says we always have a choice."

"Well maybe Natalie's had a relatively lucky life. Perhaps she's never been a victim of circumstance or ever had to battle with personal demons."

"Your main demon being your father?"

"And the tidal wave he left behind."

"What happened to your father, anyway?" I ask, relieved that for the first time Alexandre's opening up about his past. I need to strike while the iron's hot – I may not get this opportunity again.

"He disappeared."

"Really?"

The look on Alexandre's face is a chilling mask when he says, "Yes, really, Pearl. The nasty piece of shit just disappeared into thin air."

"Aren't you worried he could re-surface one day? I mean, not that he could hurt you now that you're a grown man, but psychologically speaking. He could come back to haunt you in some way."

"No. He won't come back. He's gone for good."

"How can you be so sure? Sometimes when you think something's buried it can come back with a vengeance just when you least expect it."

"Because as far as I'm concerned, that bastard's buried for good." Alexandre's eyes are cold fire, the green in them flicker to a pale, icy gold and for just a second I feel as if I'm looking into the gaze of a man capable of murder.

8

Two days have passed. I've been working with Alessandra at her house in Topanga Canyon. Her attitude has changed. She's less cocky than when we first met, as if she had something to prove then – as if she felt competitive with Alexandre in some way. Since that first day, she hasn't been coming on to me or flirting. Thank God. We've made huge headway with the script. She has a sharp sense of humor and has managed to slip in a lot of great one-liners. They still haven't chosen her leading man – everything is up in the air while Sam awaits decisions from tough-cookie agents and managers. Whatever, whoever, the actor will be a star. If this film is successful, I'll get a nice percentage of the box-office. This is a win-win situation for all of us.

I've been so busy that I haven't had a chance to speak to anyone about my nightmares.

When I get back to the hotel after a full day's work, I call

Daisy. I need her sound advice. It's strange – when you get older you become more and more picky about who you spend time with and in whom you confide. I used to wear my heart on my sleeve and had never since associated bottling up my feelings with that dreaded night. But when I think about it, it was after that that everything changed – when I lost my trust in people. I had never put two and two together. Because I had not been aware, until now, of how it affected me psychologically.

I lie back on my deliciously comfortable hotel bed leaning against the padded headrest and I stretch out my legs. Daisy takes a long time to pick up.

"Amy stop that," she finally shouts into the receiver.

"Daisy?"

"Oh, hi Pearl. Sorry, Amy's being all needy right now. One sec. Amy - if you want my attention then you need to sit quietly with your coloring book for ten minutes and then we'll choose your Halloween outfit together. Is that a deal? Ten minutes only, I promise, then I'm all yours."

I can hear Amy's willful voice soften and she says, "Okay Mommy, but just ten minutes. I'm watching the clock, you know."

"Sorry about that, Pearl. Johnny's away on a business trip so she's being really demanding. He's been away a lot lately."

"I'll try to squeeze everything I have to say in ten minutes," I say jokingly.

"I know. Foolishly I taught her how to tell the time and now she's got me on a tight leash. She doesn't miss a trick."

I lay bare to Daisy the details about my nightmares and how I've been keeping their content a secret from Alexandre - bearing in mind, I let her know, about what she said about him being a

'Latin man at heart.'

"Okay, Pearl, first off, since we had that conversation in my office? Things are not the same as I had previously imagined."

I plump another cushion behind my head. "What d'you mean?" I ask - sure that whatever advice she gives me will be sound.

"Well, how you are describing the situation now colors things very differently. You'd always led me to believe that you had been totally up for that threesome with the two footballers but you were so out of it, that later, you couldn't remember what happened."

"Yeah, well that's still true. I mean, it's only since these flashbacks - these dreams, that I realize there was more to the whole story."

"This is what you have to figure out – were these actual *flashbacks* or are they just dreams, figments of your imagination?"

"They're so detailed, so in depth that I think it's what went down that night."

"When you confided in me years ago about this, I remember you saying that Brad found you alone in the boys' room drunk as a skunk, naked in a stranger's bed with used condoms strewn about and vomit all over the bedclothes. And he freaked out but took you home and then, basically, never spoke to you again and that was the end of your relationship."

"That's what I thought. I mean, yes, that's what happened afterwards when he found me, but before that I can't be sure what took place. At the time it was just a blank. I'd blacked-out."

"So now it's all coming back to you? What triggered the memory?"

"I don't know – my upcoming marriage, all that talk we had

about being honest with Alexandre and…this color…electric-blue…Rex was given an electric-blue collar and it must have just made something click – I remembered this skirt I had that was also electric-blue. I wore it that night. Something about remembering that color must have activated a part of my brain that had been shut off all that time."

"So then what happened after the third guy came through the door?"

"That's what I can't remember."

"You said your body was practically numb? Like a rag doll with no strength in your muscles?"

"Yes. I remember that clearly. I had no strength to move – I must have been really inebriated."

"Sounds like a lot more than just tequila to me."

"But I didn't smoke any weed or anything, I wasn't stoned."

"Sounds to me as if you'd been slipped some Ecstasy or something, maybe even Rohypnol or Valium."

"Ecstasy?"

"I took it once, twenty years ago. Big mistake. Well, a lot of people were doing it then, it was all the rage – I thought it would be a laugh. I remember being exactly like that, like a flopsy marionette. I couldn't move a muscle. Everybody else was dancing all night but with me it had the opposite effect. I spent the night with this guy who I thought was God's gift to the human race but when I woke up the next morning I was horrified. HORR. IF. IED."

The way Daisy tells me this with her exaggerated British accent makes me chuckle. Comic relief from a serious subject.

"That's why it's called Ecstasy," she goes on. "People are convinced they're madly in love. You see everything with rose-tinted glasses while you're high. But actually, those bastards probably gave you Valium or something. These types of drugs affect everyone differently but mixed with all those shots of tequila? You wouldn't have stood a chance, Pearl."

I twiddle my hair in thought, retracing my nightmare. "Maybe you're right…in the dream one of them said something like…what was it? Like…'It's really taking effect now.' You think they spiked my drink?"

"Hey, it happens all the time at colleges and parties, that's one of the reasons they call it 'date rape.' I *bet* they slipped something in your drink. It can cause retrograde amnesia which is obviously what happened to you. I mean, it's common for people to wake up the next morning without any memory of huge chunks of the night before. It's really rife in Britain with all this binge drinking going on with young girls. There are so many cases of fake taxi drivers raping them – you know, they get into a car thinking they're going home and end up being violated. Some even murdered. But I'm digressing – what happened to you was a classic case of date rape. Even if you had gone to the doctor for a test the next day, a lot of these date rape drugs don't even show up in urine samples."

"How d'you know all this?"

"It was part of my training. Date rape is way more common than people think and it usually goes unreported – but often it's revealed years later in therapy sessions. Like with incestual rape, people often don't want to admit to themselves that they were abused, let alone confide in someone else – it can take years to resurface sometimes. Or like with you, the victim genuinely forgets about it – blocks it out and something triggers the memory years later. It could be a smell, a word, a movie or book

– in your case it was a color that was the trigger reminding you of that skirt and everything that followed."

"The truth is, though, I asked for it, Daisy. I was dancing around in that little skirt coming on to them, flirting like crazy. And I agreed to go back to their place – they didn't force me. I was even looking forward to having a threesome. At first it seemed like a great idea."

"Oh so you think you asked to be basically, *gang raped?* This was not your fault, Pearl. This was *not* your fault. *Do you hear me?*"

"I felt so ashamed at the time and I still feel ashamed even speaking about it now."

"You and every other person who ever gets raped. It's classic – the victim feels like somehow it was their fault and they were asking for it. Their lipstick was too bright, the skirt too short, they shouldn't have worn high heels that evening - they should never have got into that car. The list goes on."

"The worst thing is that I suddenly feel repelled by sex – the repulsive details are all flooding back and I feel grossed out."

"That's why you need to tell Alexandre about what happened."

"But you said—"

"Pearl, that's when I thought this was about a fun, wild night out during your university years - something he really didn't need to know about. But this? This is affecting your *relationship*. This is a whole different kettle of fish. It was *rape*. Just because it happened ages ago doesn't make it any less serious."

"He might think it was my fault."

"I doubt it very much. We all have a past – we've all done crazy things. This was eighteen years ago, for fuck's sake."

"Just yesterday he said how he couldn't imagine me ever

having been promiscuous or wild – he thinks I was perfect."

"Well, wakey, wakey, Alexandre Chevalier, you are engaged to be married to a mere mortal! Pearl, if he can't stomach what happened to you and if he can't deal with it in an adult way then you really shouldn't be marrying him anyway. Listen, Amy says my time is up and I don't like breaking promises. Call me tomorrow and we'll finish this conversation. It's good you're letting it all out, anyway."

"Bye. Thanks, Daisy, thanks for listening. Say thank you to Amy for being so generous with her mom's time."

"Please, stop making yourself sound like a bore. Of course I'm listening, This shit is serious and you need to sort through it. We'll talk tomorrow. Love you, and thank you for trusting me with all this, I know it's painful."

I get out my iPad and look up the words online that Daisy mentioned, 'retrograde amnesia.' I always thought that was a nifty trick they used in soap operas but never could have imagined it would happen to anyone in real life – to totally blank something out. At least, not unless you've had some sort of physical head trauma from a car accident or something. Although, I understand now that it *was* trauma - only mental.

If I'd remembered the course of events at the time I could have defended myself – Brad would have seen me in a different light, not as some complete slut with no morals at all. Not that having a threesome is wrong, no. But I was going steady with him. The fact that he admitted he had slept with Alicia didn't let me off the hook. I broke his heart. Broke his trust in me. We would have gotten married if he'd been able to forgive me. Maybe we would be together now.

I take a deep breath and try to stop the self-blame flooding over me. It's true what Alexandre said, that you have to accept your mistakes, the good and bad because they define who you are as a person. Perhaps if that had never happened with the footballers I wouldn't be with Alexandre today. Then again, maybe I would have had children. Who knows which path would have been the 'right' one. Are our lives destined by fate or does every single choice we make offer a gamut of possibilities like a CD with several different tracks? I chose that song, *All I Wanna Do Is Have Some Fun*...and that's where it led me that night.

I am mulling all this over and thinking about a light dinner in tonight at the hotel restaurant, when my cell rings. It's Alessandra.

Her smoky voice sounds languid and rich. She doesn't even say 'Hi, Pearl' but begins, "All we ever do is work, you and I. I think we should just hang out this evening together."

I'm taken aback. "Well, I—"

Her voice is almost a whisper. "Actually, I'm cheating. I'm already here - down in the lobby – thought I'd take a chance."

"Wow, Alessandra, what if I'd been busy?"

"I figured you'd be free. I'm on my way up to your room."

When I open the door a few minutes later, I'm stunned. It's like action replay, except the seductive person standing before me uninvited is not Alexandre but Alessandra. She stands there dressed in a clingy, silky dress – almost see-through - her nipples erect, her cascading, dark hair wild and untamed about her shoulders. She's holding a chilled bottle of Dom Pérignon and some pink roses. Déjà-vu. Except, she also holds a glass vase for the flowers.

It plops out of my mouth, "You look pretty," I say. My eyes fall on the roses. "These are for me?"

"No, they're for your alter ego, the Pearl who takes work way too seriously, the Pearl who needs a little sweetening up."

I try to stifle a grin. It's true, we've been working non-stop on the script and not spoken about anything else. "Come in, Alessandra – sorry, it's a little messy, I was just choosing something to wear. I always end up rooting through every piece of clothing I have, never knowing what to put on. I thought I'd go downstairs and eat in the hotel restaurant – the food's great here –join me if you like."

"I love this place," she says in her husky voice – "so romantic. Let's open the champagne while it's still cold. Oh look, you have a balcony, how lovely." She steps onto the balcony and surveys the ocean view. The breeze blows her dress revealing the outline of her thighs and ass. No underwear. Another thing she and Alexandre have in common. Oops, maybe we won't be dining downstairs after all; her dress is no better than a negligee. Unless I lend her a pair of my panties. No, far too intimate, perhaps room service is a better idea.

I fill up the vase Alessandra brought with water and place the flowers inside and then grab a couple of flute glasses by the mini-bar. "Thanks so much for the roses, they're beautiful."

"The rule is - this evening we won't mention the film, is that a deal?"

"It's a deal," I agree. I look at her, my eye like a camera and know that this woman is on her way to movie stardom. It's obvious. Her beauty is breathtaking. Her skin is olive-colored but flawless, an advantage these days with high definition cameras showing up every blemish. Her eyes flick up at the corners and her dark lashes are like frames making the green greener, the flecks of gold more pronounced.

She pops open the cork and some of the champagne bubbles over. She licks her fingers, her tongue slowly rimming her top lip. It's as if she and Alexandre are twins; their mannerisms are the same. Am I in the middle of a soap opera? First this retrograde amnesia business and now this. Am I about to discover that Alexandre's mother gave up one of her babies for adoption and Alexandre and Alessandra are long-lost brother and sister? She and I have been working so hard on the script, I haven't had a moment to really observe this woman but everything about her fascinates me, mostly because she reminds me of him.

We clink glasses and make a toast to the success of the film but burst out laughing simultaneously when it occurs to us that we've both broken our rule to not mention it this evening She tells me about her hybrid upbringing, that she was born in Chicago but then moved to Italy when she was six, raised in Florence by her single mom who had at that point divorced her father, an American. She spent her summer vacations with her grandparents in Sicily. She returned to the States when she was sixteen and modeled in New York before landing a commercial and an agent. Little by little, she found her way into the theatre although it was a slow progression. Finally, she got the part that won her the Tony Award and things have been going skyward from there.

She takes another sip of champagne. "The problem is I still have my Italian accent - it's hard to shake off one hundred percent."

"But it hasn't harmed your career up until now, has it? I mean, people love an accent, it makes you exotic."

"So far I've been lucky, but I want to be in the same league as Charlize."

Tough, I think. Trying to compete with the best of the best. "Well you can have elocution lessons. There must be so many voice coaches in LA. I like your accent, though. I think it would be a shame to lose it completely."

She puts her hand on my thigh. "You do?"

"Yes, I think European accents are sexy."

"Well, I suppose you would, Pearl. Tell me about your husband-to-be. Is he really as hot as he looks?"

"I thought you were gay," I reply with suspicion. *Keep away from him, femme-fatale!*

"I am. But you know what turns me on? Lying in bed with my girlfriend and watching a man fuck a woman in a porno movie. Seeing a big, hard, thick cock stretch open up a sweet tender pussy and fuck her. Or even two guys together making out."

I'm feeling the effects of the champagne and I laugh.

"Why is that funny? Didn't you know that that's a lesbian fantasy? A lot of us still love to imagine big cocks but we want to be once-removed from them, if you see what I mean." Alessandra picks up the hotel phone and nonchalantly dials room service. "Hi, can you bring us an ice-cold bottle of Dom Pérignon and some sandwiches? A mixture of snacks, I don't care, a mixture of vegetarian and whatever. Thanks."

My eyes widen. *So cocky! She didn't even ask me.*

"It's on me," she lets me know. "Now, where were we? Yes, big, huge, throbbing cocks—"

Cock…the word brings unwelcome images to my brain and I feel my eyes well with tears. The needle-dick memories flash back and a recollection of that third guy who came into the room envelops me like a blanket smothering me to suffocation. He was fat, sweaty, his penis repulsive; I remember him struggling with a condom...I cover my face with my hands in disgust – the twisting agony of what happened wrenching memories out of my body...I start hyperventilating again, my breath short. I try to suck in a lungful of air.

Alessandra steadies my shaking shoulders. "Pearl, what the hell is wrong?"

And it all comes gushing out; the whole story from beginning to end. I reveal everything to her. I'm in tears now, the memories of what happened to me thick with sordid details. The faces of the guys, how they held me down, how their repulsive penises poked and prodded as if I were nothing more than an orifice.

"The one with the fat, flaccid walnut of a penis couldn't even get it up – it made him angry," I wail in between sobs.

Alessandra is holding me in her arms. "That's right, Pearl – let it all out."

"He felt humiliated in front of his friends. There were more. I can't remember how many...but there were more. I puked up – that's when they finally left me alone. They left me there covered in vomit and semen and–"

She holds my trembling body close against her. "Now, now, my beautiful Pearl, they can't hurt you anymore."

Room service arrives and I pick at the food, hardly being able to swallow. Telling Alessandra all this was the last thing I wanted to do. So unprofessional, mixing my private life with a work situation. I should never have agreed to allow her into my hotel room, letting her look into my heart and soul. I've been an idiot.

I sit up straight and try to compose myself but I feel exhausted, spent, all my energy sucked out of me.

I don't protest when she takes control and says, "I'm going to run you a bath, Pearl, and you can just lie back and relax. Think of lovely things. Any time you have a nasty image in your mind replace it with this bunch of pink roses."

The bath is just what I need. I recline my head back, unwinding in the hot bubbly water and do as Alessandra tells me. I picture the pink roses climbing up the stone walls at Alexandre's house in Provence and the scent of lavender, the intense purple-blue of the fields, the white butterflies fluttering about like confetti. I remember the buttery croissant I ate for breakfast, the taste of homemade cherry preserve – from the cherry trees in his garden.

Alessandra puts on some music – *Woman* by Neneh Cherry – a powerful song. I close my eyes. It's healthy that all the bad memories have resurfaced but now they can go back where they came from, six feet under where they belong. It's done. It's over – I don't want the past taking over my perfect world, screwing up my life.

My lids are shut tight when I feel the bath water ripple. I open them and see two smooth, golden legs in the tub. Alessandra is joining me. *This is not what I planned!*

"Scoot over," she says, slipping herself behind me before I have a chance to object. She eases her slim body to the back of the tub and maneuvers around me so I have no choice but to lean on her, my back pressed against her breasts, her legs splayed open on either side of me. *Double déjà-vu!* But this time with her, not Alexandre.

"Use me as a cushion. Just relax," she says soothingly, pulling my shoulders back.

I'm too tired to disagree. I lean against her. She begins to lather my back with a delicious-smelling body wash as she sings along to the song…about being a woman's world. Her hands are firm but soft as she massages my shoulders with her fingertips, kneading out the knots – the stress.

"This feels good," I tell her, realizing it's past the point of protesting. Anyway, who cares? What's the worst that can happen? Alexandre said himself he wouldn't mind. She's a woman – she can't hurt me. A little rubdown can't be a bad thing.

She continues with this wonderful massage for a good ten minutes. I'm like putty in her agile hands. Then her fingers run themselves from my shoulders to my front and tantalizingly across my breasts. She isn't touching the nipples, just circling around and around – all part of her skillful massage. But my body does things my conscience can't control: my nipples pucker and to my surprise I'm silently begging for her to tweak them – the massage has got me really turned-on. I don't want her to know but she senses something as her hands graze across each nipple. I feel a shooting desire connect the pulse with my core and my clit starts to throb. She begins to flutter her fingers on my nipples and I can't help it – a little moan escapes my lips and I lean back closer against her. Uh oh, that's done it.

"I thought you'd like that," she whispers, her lips grazing my ear. I shudder with secret, quiet desire. "Your tits are beautiful, Pearl. People pay thousands to get their breasts to look just like yours."

"They're real," I tell her trying to feign a normal conversation.

She flickers her pinkie seductively on one erect, rosy nipple. "Yes, I know, I can always tell."

Her hands have moved back to my shoulders and neck as she continues her soft touch. She's running the very tips of her fingers along the base of my hairline – my hair is pinned up in a messy bun. Shivers tingle through my entire body.

"I'm not gay you know, Alessandra," I blurt out, trying to convince myself that this has nothing to do with me. *I am an innocent bystander in all this!*

"No," she murmurs, "of course not, but who's going to arrest you, huh? Just relax, I'm just giving you a little massage, that's all. You're holding in a lot of tension."

She begins to brush my neck with her lips with whispery kisses and then her fingers are back on my nipples again. I feel the need build up inside me. Being with Alexandre has awoken my sexual appetite, a yearning for orgasms and now is no exception. She's getting me worked up. Her hand moves under the water now, searching between my thighs. My breath gasps in anticipation. *I don't want her to stop… yet this is…wrong!*

My conscious mind wants to tell her to leave me be but I can't, I'm simply too turned-on. Her finger taps my clit gently making me flex my hips. I want more and she can sense that. Oh yes, she can sense it alright. She presses her palm flat on my Venus and the pressure of it has me moving up against her hand. She makes circular motions almost imperceptibly but it's just enough to feel myself throb as if my heartbeat were right down there. With the other hand she tugs at my nipple, kneading it softly between her fingers. She slips her index finger from her right hand inside my slick opening, continuing with the pressure on my clit.

"I'm not gay," I repeat, sensations unspooling, my hips grinding on her hand in a ripple of carnal desire, "but this does…aah…oh yeah…feel…so…good."

"Doesn't it? Your pussy's so sweet, Pearl, I'd like to flicker my tongue against your clit." She presses her hand harder on my purring V-8 now and I feel myself come in a thunderous pound. My back arches as I rock my hips forward pushing on her hand - the orgasm pulsates deep inside me, her finger still there exploring my G-spot, making the double-sensation linger and flutter in waves of orgasmic bliss.

"The best way to relieve tension is through climax," she says quietly. "If you ever have a migraine you know what to do."

Sensations of shameful bliss are still pulsing through me, my clit tingling with aftershocks, the base of me beautifully released. *I am not a lesbian! How has this happened?* "Alessandra, this was a one-off. I can't let this happen again."

But she just laughs. "Don't be so serious, Pearl. It's just a release, that's all. Your body needed it."

"I'm not going to reciprocate," I warn her. I can't see her expression as she's behind me but I can imagine it. I have a picture in my mind's eye of a cool smirk etched across her beautiful face.

And it scares me.

No woman has touched me like this. Ever.

And I'm shocked at how I responded with so much desire.

I awake to the sound of the Skype ring on my iPad and hazily turn on my side. I didn't have any nightmares last night, I had night mares, or should I say, a night of *mares*. No stallions. I dreamed about females - beautiful breasts, slender long legs. *This is crazy!* Still, I guess it's better that visions of women erase the grotesque, panting images of what was there before.

Ugh, I can't even think about it.

I unlock my tablet. It's Alexandre.

I quietly recount my adventure yesterday evening – I'm wondering if he'll be as delighted as he said he'd be. Perhaps he might get jealous.

But no - jealousy doesn't seem to hold a place with him when a woman is involved. He responds huskily, "If my plane wasn't about to take off right now, I'd want a full recount of every single, tiny, sexy detail and I'd pleasure myself while you recounted each horny moment. I swear to God you've got me all worked up thinking about it."

I can hear the jet's engines roaring in the background. "I'm not proud of what I did," I say tentatively. "It just sort of….unfolded. It won't happen again, I promise."

"Pearl, have some fun, don't take it all so seriously."

I freeze. Isn't that exactly what *she* said? "I have something really important to tell you. Something that's been responsible for my bad dreams….hello?…Alexandre?"

The line's gone dead. I call him back on both Skype and his cell number. Nothing.

I roll out of bed and amble to the bathroom. I miss Alexandre – it strikes me that all I really want to do is be with him and Rex, cozy together watching a movie or a walk in the park. Work used to be so important to me but now less so. I mull over the 'lady of leisure' fantasy he sold me yesterday, lying by the beach reading novels. Or the pair of us escaping to Thailand and living in a tree-house – leaving the 'real' world behind. Usually when you cook up a fantasy it's unattainable but for us it could be a reality. A sweet thought. But the Devil makes work for idle hands, doesn't he?

With this in mind I shower quickly, get myself ready and set off for work in my outrageous low and vast, powder blue Cadillac that feels like a ship. I swing by my favorite smoothie stall feeling cruel that I blamed it for my 'food poisoning.' In a few hours I'll be able to speak to Alexandre and we can have a long talk. I want to get these dreams off my chest, I want to lay it all open – I'm sick of harboring this secret.

As I cruise along Pacific Coast Highway, sipping my strawberry smoothie, I wonder if I could adapt to this city – smoothies, the ocean, palm trees swaying in a warm breeze, beautiful people everywhere – what isn't there to love?

This is my last day with Alessandra – our last day working on the script. I have to admit that it's been fun but right now the last thing I need is the possibility of more complications. It was a highly pleasurable one-off experience in the bathtub but I mustn't let her have her seductive way again. *Watch out Pearl, be on your guard.*

It's cooler today so we write inside. We settle in the living room, which is an extension of her open-plan kitchen. The place is decorated with Navajo hand-woven rugs and an eclectic mix of oil paintings that are copies of Klimt and Frida Kahlo. There's a wood-burning stove in the corner with a brick surround and bookcases stuffed with self-help books and…dare I say it, Russian novels. Spooky…a woman after my own heart.

"You have the same reading taste as me," I remark, setting down my bag and sitting on a big arm chair.

"I knew we'd think alike, Pearl. We're mirrors of each other."

I want to tell her that she's the female image of Alexandre, not me, but I say nothing. The less we talk about my fiancé, the better.

She pulls back her long, dark hair into a ponytail, settles cross-legged on the sofa and says, "I told you so much about my life, my family in Italy and stuff but you've revealed nothing about yourself."

Only the most personal thing ever. "Oh, my life has been very normal," I hedge. "You know, school in New York, college, jobs, marriage, divorce, and now I'm engaged."

"Engaged to one of the richest men in the world."

"Well, I don't focus on that aspect. Money doesn't motivate me."

"What does motivate you, Pearl?"

"Passion. In work. In love. In ideas. I think you have to really believe in what you do on every level. You know, morally and spiritually speaking."

"Do you believe in *Stone Trooper?*"

Her question grabs me by the throat. Do I believe in this Hollywood blockbuster? Is it important on the grand scale of things? Or is what Natalie is doing so much more significant? "Of course I do," I reply with a half lie. "I mean, I think the fact that your character Sunny is gay is important. A movie with a message. So many people are homophobic."

"Are you homophobic, Pearl?"

"No! Of course not. I believe in gay rights, I believe in same-sex marriage, I believe in—"

"You kept trying to convince me last night that you weren't gay. Why is it okay with you that others are gay but not yourself?"

"But I—"

"Why label things? Why is it so important for you to limit yourself, to pigeon-hole yourself?"

"I….I…" I stammer, "I guess I've never thought of myself as being locked in some pigeon-hole." For some strange reason I feel hurt by her accusation. *I am liberal-minded!*

Her voice softens at my injured expression. "You're so tender, Pearl. So vulnerable. I hope your husband-to-be realizes how lucky he is."

"He tells me every day."

She locks her eyes with mine and says quietly, "When you came by my hand yesterday in the bath, I could feel you tremble, feel your beautiful little pussy-pearl quiver – you know, just the thrill of it, the excitement gave me an orgasm too."

But how? You didn't even touch yourself.

She goes on in her husky voice, "All I had to do was give myself a tight clench and I felt little ripples of pleasure. Not a bumper-big, mind-blowing orgasm but, you know…a little thrill. Touching your hard nipples and those beautiful boobs of yours – seeing how turned on I got you…well…you got me horny, Pearl." She bites her lower lip. "My pussy flutters a little when you look at me with your big blue eyes. But you know that, don't you? You know you penetrate me with your intense, come-on stare, don't you?"

"Alessandra! I'm not trying to seduce you!"

She chortles with laughter. "Just kidding. Where's your sense of humor? Lighten up."

I sigh with relief but am alarmed when I can sense my panties have got a little moist after what she just said. I shuffle my position on the couch and sit up straight. "We need to finish this script," I say assertively. "I'm leaving tomorrow morning."

She pouts her full red lips. "Such a shame. We've had so much fun together."

I spend the next twenty minutes with my legs firmly crossed listening to what Alessandra has to say about *Stone Trooper* and the ideas she has for the love scenes. Somehow, she has convinced Sam that a full-on sex scene between her and her onscreen girlfriend in the film is a must. "To titillate the audience," she explains.

I have Lucifer purring away on my knees while I'm also trying to type on my laptop. I look up. "Alessandra, there's no way our kind of audience will be up for that."

"Oh, stop being so backward-thinking. People are more open-minded these days. Mid-American housewives are reading about bondage and sex toys for God's sake – hell, they're even experimenting with it all."

"Yes, but *gay* sex in a mainstream movie? A blockbuster, buddy movie?"

"Why not?"

"Because, because…"

"It hasn't been done before?"

"No, I don't think it has. This is not some French or Italian art-house film. This will be screened in shopping malls across the USA."

"Then give them something to talk about with their popcorn and soda."

I put my laptop aside and gently unhook Lucifer's claws from my skirt. I get off the couch and stretch my arms. "I'm going to have to talk to Sam about this, Alessandra. Personally, I don't think it will work. I mean, I know that gay characters in movies are either marginalized or made the punch-line for degrading jokes a lot of the time and so having your character being gay, and you, yourself, being gay, is already a big leap forward. We can hint at sex, show a kiss or something but a full-on lesbian love scene?"

"I thought a little light BDSM."

I laugh. "Okay, now I know you're kidding me. It's that crazy Italian sense of humor. You Europeans - really. Alexandre does the same thing to me...you know, that poker face thing? Which is what you're doing now. Very funny. You guys are expert at getting us Americans all worked up for nothing."

I think back to that time when Alexandre tied my ankles to the bedpost when he said I'd been disrespectful and needed to be punished – his wacky sense of humor had me fooled at first.

As if reading my mind, Alessandra says, "I think we should play it out. Do a little improv acting – we thespians love that."

I burst out laughing at her unintentional (or perhaps intentional) onomatopoeia with the word, thespian. "Lesbian bondage?"

She still dons her poker face. "Yes, why not?"

"Not even my fiancé would approve of that."

She widens her eyes innocently. "He's not into a little dominance play? A little S&M? He looks the type. So manly...so controlling Alpha male."

"No way. He won't come near me with a whip. Personally, it's something I wouldn't mind experimenting with - but him? Not a chance."

She rolls her eyes. "My ex girlfriend is like that. Can't play Dom and Sub with her ever – she has an aversion to any kind of physical power play. Except, I think in the past she's got pretty tough with men. You know when she was kinda straight. But she would never lay a hand on me."

"Yeah, well, in my fiancé's case, he has good reason. A

violent childho—" *Shut up, Pearl!* I stop my sentence midway and change the subject. "Who did these paintings on the wall? They're lovely copies. Got the colors just right."

"I did."

I raise my eyebrows. "You're an artist as well as an actress? Why does that not surprise me?"

I wander about the room feeling extremely uneasy. I promised Sam we'd get this script done and dusted but now I'm feeling like I want out of this part of the project altogether. This whole movie process is giving me the willies. Something about it just doesn't seem right. The procedure doesn't feel normal...both of us tinkering about with the script and we're not the official script writers. Then again, having only ever worked on documentaries, who am I to judge? This is Hollywood, not a world I know well.

"Do'you mind if I make us some coffee?" I ask, stalling my decision as to whether I should throw in the towel and let her get on with it with the script doctor. I don't have time to play her silly games right now, nor second guess what's going on in her nutty mind. Besides, I find her disconcertingly attractive, mixed with my anti-male mind-set after my needle-dick nightmares – I'm an easy target right now. I don't want to succumb to her sexual charms again.

Alessandra gets up, the folds of her dress falling like ripples of water about her willowy body "Let me help you."

"No, really, I can do it. You relax. You take sugar, don't you?"

"Just half a teaspoon."

"Sure."

I slip off to the kitchen, relieved to get away from her for a moment and her quirky, oddball demeanor. I take two funky pottery mugs down from a shelf. They look like they were hand-painted by a child. I turn on the coffee percolator. The kitchen is chaotic. There are piles of scripts and baskets of fruit also stuffed with stray papers, magazines and bills. Lucifer comes in and jumps on the kitchen table, his tail up vertically swishing from side to side. He leaps across to the kitchen counter landing on a pile of papers in one of the baskets which he then begins to use to sharpen his claws. "Lucifer, you naughty boy." I prize his paws away from the basket and take him in my arms. But something catches my attention. A name.

Sophie Dumas.

My heart is beating fast. It's a business letter about *Stone Trooper* from Samuel Myers to Alessandra.

Producers: Sophie Dumas / HookedUp Enterprises.

Executive producer: Samuel Myers.

Sophie is not meant to be involved with this project! In any shape or form. I stand there for a moment staring at the letter, a rush of blood pumping in my ears – I can feel myself redden with fury. This must be some sort of mistake.

I march into the living room, still with Lucifer in my arms and say to Alessandra. "Who is the producer on this movie?"

She sits up and looks at me surprised. "Sam Myers with HookedUp Enterprises."

"He's the Producer or executive producer?"

"Oh, you must have seen some paperwork in the kitchen."

"Yes. I wasn't snooping. Lucifer landed on a very interesting piece of information which I - as co-producer and director of HookedUp Enterprises…" I stop myself short. This is so unprofessional. Alessandra has been hired as an actress – she doesn't need to know about this cock-up. It makes me look incompetent to be so in the dark. To have been hoodwinked like this. To have been such a frigging, freaking *idiot*.

"Do you know Sophie Dumas?" I ask, trying to sound casual.

"I know who she is and we once spoke on the phone. She's one of the producers of *Stone Trooper*. I mean co-producer with Sam and HookedUp Enterprises – you're partners, aren't you? I mean, HookedUp Enterprises is Sophie Dumas and Alexandre Chevalier fifty/fifty, isn't it?"

I want to scream. I want to shout out, *No, actually, that meddling bitch is not part of HookedUp Enterprises at all.* I can feel my knees trembling but I try to stay calm. "The coffee sounds like it's ready. One sugar, you said?"

"Half a teaspoon."

"Oh yes, that's right." I set the cat down and go back to the kitchen. I cradle my head in my hands and wonder what I should do next.

I need to see Samuel Myers - find out what the hell is going on.

9

It takes a while to park my shark of a car in the garage of Samuel Myers office building Downtown. I haven't warned him of my arrival in case he detects the anger in my voice. I have been duped – I need to get to the bottom of this without losing my cool. If that's possible. Once I've got an answer from him I'll call my sweet sister-in-law to find out what the fuck she's playing at. On second thoughts, no. I won't give her the satisfaction. I don't want her knowing that she's getting to me.

And then I'll call Alexandre.

I take the elevator up to the seventh floor. I was not prepared for this. I look very casual in just a pair of jeans, T-shirt and Converse sneakers. I'm not even wearing make-up; I wanted to dress down for Alessandra, to try and keep her advances at bay.

I needn't be worried, though. The receptionist and everyone at his office is very laid-back, LA style, although a little put out that I don't have an appointment. I'm in luck. Sam is here, just finishing up a long distance call, they tell me. The setting is not as grand as I had imagined and a little dated with big old couches and a wooden and glass coffee table piled with out of date magazines. They offer me a drink and I glug down a glass of water – the heat I feel inside needs to be quenched. I sit there flicking through an old Vanity Fair. I hear a door open and I look up.

Sam waddles towards me – his smile beaming as if he's delighted to see me. He ushers me ahead of him into his office, pulling the door closed behind him. The book shelves are lined with movies and there is an Academy Award in prime position. There are family photos in gold frames on his large desk and at one end of the room a basketball net. I can just imagine him making million dollar deals while simultaneously scoring a goal.

"Siddown, Pearl. Did they offer you a beverage?" He eases himself into his large leather swivel chair, panting with the effort.

"Yes, thank you, Mr. Myers."

"Hey, sweetheart, what's with the Mr. Myers? You look pissed."

"Well, yes, I've had quite a shock and I'd like you to explain yourself and the situation. Perhaps there's been a typo on a letter I saw. I'm hoping that I'm completely wrong, hoping this has all been a mistake. However, if I am not wrong I think your prerogative to call me 'sweetheart' will be null and void."

His eyes look shifty – he twiddles his fat, caught-in-the-cookie-jar hands.

I pin my eyes on him like darts. "Please can you explain why Sophie Dumas is one of the producers?"

"Okay Pearl, firstly, she is only *technically* a producer. She is not involved in any decision making at all. Not a bit. That's just you and me. It's just money, that's all. She's fronting the money – she's a silent partner, so to speak."

"So to speak? So to lie, more like."

"Hey, Pearl, nothing has changed between you and me! Sophie Dumas is not calling the shots here."

"Oh no? So if this is *her* money, not yours, she is kind of like your boss, wouldn't you say?"

"It's not like that."

"What is it like then, Mr. Myers?"

"You are the director of your company, HookedUp Enterprises but you are not the owner, am I right?"

My blood is boiling. *What has HookedUp Enterprises got to do with Sophie Dumas?* I try to remain calm. "Sophie Dumas has nothing whatsoever to do with HookedUp Enterprises, Mr. Myers. It is owned by my fiancé."

"And I signed the deal with him."

"Co-signed by me."

"Nowhere in our contract did it stipulate that I could not bring in money from my side from whatever source I chose."

"That's not true. You signed a deal saying that no backers would be involved in politically incorrect dealings –"

"Sophie Dumas is not laundering dirty money, Pearl. Hey, she's your sister-in-law, what's the big deal? She told me you two were close."

"Don't bullshit me, Sam. If we were so close you wouldn't be red in the face from embarrassment right now. You would have been straight with me."

"What was the point of telling you? Money is money. The point is, the movie is going to get made – we have the money.

You will make a lot from this - you still get your cut just the same - your percentage. Nothing has changed, Pearl, sweetheart.

"My trust in you – that's what's changed."

"Okay, okay, I admit it. I screwed up - I should have let you know sooner. But she only just came on board a while ago. I've been having a rough patch and she came along at the perfect moment. She's bailing out my ass. I had an unexpected loss on a project recently – as far as I'm concerned, Sophie's doing us all a big favor. Your fiancé isn't upset about this so why should you be?"

I feel as if I've just been hit over the head with a baseball bat. *Alexandre already knows about this??* I need to get information so I can't let him know that this is such a shock. "What were Alexandre's words to you exactly? And at what point did you discuss this?"

"Just after he landed back in New York. The other day, I guess."

"I see."

"He told me it was best if he discussed it with you first. That's why I didn't mention it to you, Pearl. You know, I didn't want to get out my big wooden spoon and stir about someone else's family affairs."

I notice my fists are scrunched into balls as my nails are digging into my hands. I say between my teeth, "You and I are business partners – we are meant to tell each other about anything that could affect this movie. This is not some freaking *family affair*! I resent that you just said that!"

"Calm down, Pearl."

"No, I won't calm down! I could sue you for breach of contract. I won't because I don't want to waste my time and energy but this is the last time you will be doing business with HookedUp Enterprises. I will finish this movie because I'm a professional. The show *will* go on. But I do not want to have one single meeting with Sophie Dumas. Is that clear? I do not want to hear her name, nor see her at the premiere. If I so much get an inkling of her rootling about my business I will get my lawyers on to you. You are a powerful man, Mr. Myers, but my fiancé is even more powerful and richer than you are."

His eyes look down ashamedly.

"By the way," I spit out, "I don't want Sophie knowing that we've had this conversation. I don't want you running off tittle-tattling to her about what a bitch I've been."

"You can count on it, I won't say a word."

"What you did was wrong. It wasn't unethical. It was sneaky and dishonest."

He smiles at me weakly. "Welcome to Hollywood, Pearl."

I take the flamboyant powder blue Cadillac back to the car hire and swap it for a BMW. I don't want to advertise my whereabouts to the whole of LA. I go to the hotel and check out and call the airline to cancel my flight to New York.

I will not be returning home tomorrow. I'm not sure what I should do now – I need to come up with a plan. Sitting in my new rental car in a parking lot near Santa Monica Pier, I call Alexandre. Over the phone is hardly the best way to manage problems in a relationship but I have had enough. I cannot live my life with mistrust. I cannot have this as-good-as incestuous relationship between him and his freaky sister barging in on me with every breath I take. He knew about Sophie producing *Stone Trooper* and he didn't call to let me know! I'll give him a chance to explain himself but if he doesn't come up with an airtight answer, then that's it.

It's her or me.

He cannot have us both. He will have to choose. Now. Not tomorrow, not 'when the time is right but – N.O.W.

I need to have this resolved or nothing will ever change. This is the most painful thing I have ever done in my life but I have no choice. If I don't stand firm now, this Sophie nonsense will never end.

Shaking, I press in his number. His plane will have landed by now.

"Hello?" he says. Just hearing his deep, melodic voice has me trembling all the more. I am so in love with this man. But I am so furious with him, too.

Without saying 'hi' I screech out, "Why didn't you tell me, Alexandre?"

"Nice to hear your voice, chérie. What's up?"

"What's up is that I have just come out of a meeting with Samuel Myers. Nice to be working on a movie where I am the last person to find something out. And I say, *find something out*, as in, not be enlightened by people around me whom I am meant to trust, one of those people being my *fiancé*," I cry out, my voice rising as I splutter out that last word.

"Calm down, Pearl. I was going to tell you when the time was right."

"If you use this 'time-is-right' crap on me anymore I'll–"

"I was going to call you right now, in fact. It totally slipped my mind, chérie. I just didn't think it was *that* important because the source of where the money was coming from was not going to affect you in anyway personally."

"What is *wrong* with you? This is meant to be a HookedUp Enterprises project. That is the *whole point!* HookedUp *Enterprises* is not part of HookedUp. This is not supposed to have anything to do with your sister *at all!*"

"It's just money, Pearl. Nothing more. I've already spoken to her about it. She swears she won't get involved in the creative side. Sam Myers is in financial straits."

"You know what? I wouldn't be surprised if that's all a big fabrication – an excuse for Sophie to wheedle her way into my business. Because one minute Samuel Myers is one of the most powerful producers in Hollywood and suddenly he's in a quagmire and Sophie just happens to bail him out at the perfect moment – sounds very fishy to me."

"Pearl, you're reading way too much into this. He was in a bad way and, yes, maybe Sophie saw a good business opportunity and she snapped it up. She's getting a chunk of his company in exchange. In the long term it could be a great deal for her."

"Well bully for her! But it is not a great deal for *me!* Or, I might add, for our future marriage. Or should I say, to be more precise, our *ex*-future marriage!" I am stumbling now, spurting nonsense but I mean every word of my jumbled phrases, however higgledy-piggledy they come out.

There is silence. *Has he hung up on me?*

"Alexandre?"

I can hear his breathing. "You don't mean that, baby. We're going ahead with this wedding and nothing's going to stop me. Sophie's separate from all this. You have got to stop obsessing about her and just ignore her."

"Me obsessing about *her?* I think you'll find it's the other way round, Alexandre. You know what? That's *it.* I thought maybe we had a chance to sort this problem out but I see that you are not budging – stubborn as ever. You are so fucking wrapped up and wrapped around your older sister's devious little finger that you might as well be fucking her for all I care. You two can carry on and live happily ever after because I'm *out.* OUT! Do you hear me? Our relationship is over! I love you but I do not love her and I do not want her burrowing her way into our marriage. You said you were working on ways of extricating yourself from her with HookedUp and in your personal life. Like a fool I believed you. I trusted you. But it was all *bullshit!*"

"Pearl, please, darling stop. I know she had good reason to do what she did. She–"

"Alexandre, you can make excuses till the cows come home. I am not going to listen anymore. If the day ever, ever comes when you and she are one hundred percent separated businesswise, then give me a call. Meanwhile, we are over. I am not returning to New York. I'll finish *Stone Trooper* from a distance by email and long distance calls. Once I have started a project I don't think it's professional to abandon ship. However, after that…well I don't know yet…I'll need to work that through but–"

"I'm coming to Los Angeles tonight to get you. This is crazy. We're getting married. We'll get married in Vegas tomorrow and we can do the white wedding, too, if you want. I'm not standing for this, Pearl. I give you my word I'll dissolve my part of HookedUp. I'll make it go public or Sophie can buy me out but it will take time, I can't do something like that overnight. We can draw up a contract with lawyers if you don't believe me."

"Oh, like the HookedUp Enterprises contract we drew up? Fat lot of good that did! Sophie found a little loophole to slip her way in like the sly snake she is!"

"You're not listening to reason, Pearl, so I'm coming to get you. I'm calling on my other cell right now and cancelling my meeting here in Montreal. I'm turning around as we speak. I'll hire a jet and come right now to LA. We'll go to Vegas and—"

"You're not listening to me, are you? You deal with your sister and HookedUp *first* and when you can prove to me that it is *finished,* signed, sealed and delivered, then give me a call. Until then, adieu, Alexandre." And I add with a tone of spite in my voice, "Besides, the last thing I want is to have a relationship with a *penis* right now."

His voice is incredulous, tight with anger. "*Excuse* me? Is that what I am to you? A *penis?*"

"Men are pigs. All of you. Deep down inside all you do is rule your lives by your dicks! You rape women. You even rape babies to 'cure' yourselves of AIDS which, hello, you got from fucking prostitutes in the first place – underage, abused prostitutes who should be in school or playing with dolls—"

"What has that got to do with me? What are you *talking* about?"

"The rape ratio in South Africa? One in four men there have committed rape!"

"Pearl—"

"Oh, and that sick, pedophile British DJ who's dead now? Have you heard about him on the news? Men are sticking their dicks everywhere – they have been since time immemorial - they don't care who they hurt both physically and mentally – children, disabled people - as long as they get themselves and their stinking

140

dicks off!"

He replies softly to my accusations, "My darling, where's all this coming from? *What* is going on?"

I'm weeping now, yowling. I sound like a braying donkey as I suck in air between sobs, my head resting on the steering wheel, my body shaking. I manage to get out, "I can't talk about this anymore. Call Daisy, she'll... tell you... what...h...happened... to...m.... me."

I hang up. I can't even think straight. Here I am sitting in my parked rental car with nowhere to go. I can't return to New York right now – I've sublet my apartment. I need a break from Alexandre. Okay, I know, I'm being dramatic – even childish. But it is the only way of getting it through his head. *I do not want Sophie in my life!* Why can't he get that? The one thing I hung onto was my autonomy, my work. And even *that* she is trying to snatch away from me.

My cell goes. It's him. It keeps ringing. I let my blood simmer a little, dry my eyes, take a deep breath and pick up.

His voice is steady. "I've cancelled my meeting. I'm on my way."

"Don't do that because I won't be here when you arrive."

I can hear the clipping sound of his purposeful footsteps. He's talking in motion, his long legs striding towards his goal which happens to be me right now. "Stay where you are, Pearl. You're being absurd."

"I need some time to think all this through. I don't want to see you for a while, Alexandre."

He sighs. The anguish in his voice is palpable. "What happened to you? It's about those nightmares, isn't it? What happened, baby? Please tell me. Please trust me."

I close my eyes and draw my knees up to my chest, and sink into the seat of the car. "A long time ago when I was at university…" I break my sentence.

"Go on, baby. I'm here for you. I love you," he cajoles. "Please, share your pain with me. Your pain is my pain. I can help. I can help you through this."

"No, you can't. You're a guy. I'm disgusted by men right now."

"I understand. I swear I do. I know that men can be vile. You don't think I know that after my father? But we aren't all bad, Pearl. We can be kind and caring. What happened, my angel? Please," he begs gently.

"I was… gang raped," and I add quickly, "but I asked for it. I wore a micro-mini skirt. I went back to their room willingly – I thought it would be fun, me with two guys. I invited it to happen, Alexandre. But it turned into something else. Something sick and gross."

I can hear the echoey announcements at Montreal airport and Alexandre's quiet breathing. I knew it. The idea of me behaving like a slut is too much for him, even if it happened eighteen years ago.

"Who did this to you?"

"You think I remember? I blanked out. I blocked it out. All this shit has been resurfacing in dreams. I can't even prove it happened. I was zonked out - drunk. Daisy thinks they may have spiked my tequila. Who knows? I behaved like a slut and I got raped."

His voice is edgy: "You did *not*," and he says between gritted teeth, "behave like a slut."

"Thank you," I reply quietly.

142

"We'll get through this together. We don't have to make love, baby. I won't touch you, I promise. Not until you're ready."

"Please don't come, Alexandre. I'm serious about what I said. Deal with Sophie and HookedUp first. I need some time alone. I'll call you in…like…a week or something. Bye."

I switch off my cell and take a deep breath. If any of this is to work between us I want Sophie out of our lives. Poor Alexandre – he's being understanding…but still. He is part of the male species and for now I don't want a penis near me bringing back visions of needle and walnut-dicks. I need some time to myself.

I get out of the car and start strolling towards Santa Monica Pier. The sun is setting - the sky swirling in moody blues, streaked with orange, making shimmering reflections on the ocean. To the north, the view of the Malibu mountains is spectacular. I walk briskly until I arrive at the pier. A trapeze school, The Trapeze School New York, is offering classes to anyone daring enough. Their logo reads, *Forget fear. Worry about the addiction.* Hmm….addiction. That is how I felt about Alexandre - completely addicted to him. But now that the sexual craving has waned on my part – at least for now – how will that affect our relationship? Before, when there was a problem we worked it out through sex. The infatuation and carnal desire we held for one another was so all-consuming, so powerful, it overrode everything. Will that need and desire return? The compulsion to have him inside me? Fucking me at every opportunity? Right now I need space, freedom. I can't bear the idea of being smothered, my body invaded - even by him.

My cell is off. He'll be frantically phoning now. I feel cruel. But then I remember Sophie again slithering into our lives in her oh-so-subtle way.

I watch one of the trapeze students, a little girl who can't be more than eight-years-old - swinging back and forth high above me and I'm tempted to give it a go myself. Anything to clear my mind of its present turmoil.

I ask the young woman standing there, "I guess all the classes must be booked up way in advance?"

"Well actually, someone just cancelled. Lost his nerve."

"Could I take his place?"

"Sure. Have you ever done this before?"

"Only in my dreams."

She laughs. "Well, now you can know what it's like to fly for real. You wanna try?"

"I sure do."

I whip out my credit card, pay and sign a waiver agreeing to take full responsibility for my own risk.

She instructs me, "Okay, you'll need to tie up your hair in a ponytail and have you got anything other than jeans to wear? Something more comfortable that gives you room to move better?"

"I have some yoga pants in my handbag."

"Perfect. You can put them on behind here." She leads me around to the side where there is a makeshift changing room.

This is crazy. Here I am in the middle of some existential crisis and I'm about to risk my life on a trapeze. Actually, that's a wild exaggeration – there's a safety net to catch my fall but I guess anything could happen or they wouldn't have asked me to sign that waiver. I'll be upside down, hooked onto the bar with my knees, swinging back and forth until the 'catcher' can get me, our hands linking. It'll take a few goes but let's see if I can be as good as that child up there.

When it comes to my turn I climb the ladder in my harness and stand on the platform about twenty-three feet up. I feel vertigo but am determined to go ahead with it. I look out over the dark blue ocean and the streaky sky. It's cooler up here, a light breeze catches me and the nervy heat I'm feeling inside is momentarily at bay. My heart is thumping – I feel so high up.

A topless man wearing what look like white pajama bottoms hooks the trapeze with a pole and brings it towards me. He connects another rope to my front. Uh, oh, here we go. I launch out into the air pushing my legs forward horizontally with great momentum and then hook them above my head, under and around the bar. This is scary. I have the choice to stay doubled up or let go. Will my legs be strong enough to hold me? After a few seconds, I do let go and feel my arms and torso drop like a big lead weight. I am completely upside down. I haven't done this sort of thing since fourth grade! The woman below me is screaming instructions, "forward, backwards, forward, backwards," and I swing my legs like a pendulum. Then I drop myself into the net. End of go one.

I wait my next turn, adrenaline pumping and wish Alexandre were here to share this experience with me. It reminds me of our first date together when we went rock-climbing. He'd be proud of me now. My cell is in my purse in the trapeze school's office. I can't call him now. Should I later? Or just leave it? I need him to know I'm serious about Sophie. I must remain strong or the next forty years of marriage or as long as we all live, will be one frustrating-as-hell compromise.

After a few more turns on the trapeze, taking my turn between the eight year-old girl, a couple of surfer dudes and another woman around my age, I manage to do the swinging circus 'catch.' Hooray!

This whole experience has given me a sense of strength.

I walk back to my car. The sun has set for the evening leaving the sky a deep cobalt blue - a lone star is flickering on the horizon and I make a wish. Star light star bright, first star I see tonight... *I wish that Sophie would get the hell out of our lives for good.*

An overriding feeling of emotion hits me and I start crying again.

Alexandre said he's on his way to get me. But the only man I can bear spending time with right now is my father.

I need my dad. I make a snap decision.

Kauai here I come.

10

I decide it's only fair to swing by Alessandra's to say goodbye and explain the situation. She's going to get wind of it one way or another so I might as well inform her that I won't be returning to LA for meetings – that I'll be emailing and Skyping, if need be, but distancing myself emotionally from the movie project. What I thought was 'my baby' now has a surrogate mother:

Sophie Dumas.

I've been betrayed on so many levels and it has made me bitter towards Hollywood. It has brought something to light: I want my old job back - I feel the urge to do documentaries again. I don't care about movie stars and big budgets. I care about those little Nigerian girls who are being sold for sexual slavery. I care about the fourteen year-old girl Malala, shot in the head by a Taliban man for championing education for girls. By some miracle she's still alive.

These are the things that drive my passion. Not some blockbuster, even if it does have a gay rights message.

I call Alessandra just to make sure she's going to be in. And on my way I swing by a Thai restaurant and pick up some Tom Yam soup and other treats. I'm hungry after my trapeze exertion and I'm sure Alessandra will be up for a bit of Thai food.

She is. When I walk into her house I realize that I haven't been here before when it's dark. She has lit her wood-burning stove and it smells of firewood and rose incense. She's delighted that I brought take-out and we begin to heat up the soup as we stand in the kitchen chatting.

She's wearing tight jeans and I can't help my roving eye. Women are always checking out each other's buns – but I'm not comparing myself to her; I'm admiring her sexy curves. I can't help it. I myself, though, still look a bit disheveled and truthfully need a shower. I know I look anything but hot.

"You wanna watch a movie or you want to talk about *Stone Trooper?* she asks, stirring the Tom Yam.

"You know what? I'm a bit Troopered-out."

I reveal to her the whole Sophie saga, keeping the tale simple and not too dramatic but explaining why I'll be bowing out gracefully from any more script tweaking and future get-togethers. I tell her about my plan to see my father and that I'm flying to Hawaii tomorrow morning.

"I'll miss you," she says, her eyes mournful. "So it's your last night at that cool hotel, huh?"

"Actually I checked out. I was in a flustered state, I thought I might be getting on a plane that very second but then I got distracted by the trapeze school on Santa Monica Pier."

"Oh so that's what the sweaty appearance is? I wondered why

you were looking so mussed up."

"Would you mind if I took a shower?"

"Sure, of course. You wanna eat now or wait?"

"I'll take a quick shower first, why not – I don't want to stink up the kitchen."

She gets out some plates from a cupboard. "I like the smell of your sweat. It's sexy."

I snigger sarcastically. "Now that *has* to be a lie."

"No it's not. My ex…well she goes crazy for underarms, you know?"

"Well I have to admit, I like the smell of Alexandre's day-old T-shirts so I do understand."

"She likes it when I have hairy armpits, it drives her wild. I mean *crazy* wild."

I grimace. "Each to their own, I guess. You're still seeing her? You refer to her as your ex yet you speak about her in the present."

She looks uneasy but doesn't answer directly. "Whenever we have….whenever we *had* a fight I'd shave to get her pissed."

I laugh. "Shaving your armpits was a big punishment?"

"I know, isn't it crazy?"

"What was she like…what is she like, your ex?"

"Beautiful. A tigress between the sheets."

"Does she live in LA?"

Alessandra looks uncomfortable. "Actually, I don't really want to talk about her, d'you mind? Let's talk about *you*, Pearl. Any more nightmares?"

I'd forgotten that I'd laid bare my soul before our bathtub 'event'. "No, no more nightmares, thank God."

"Pearl, can I ask you a very personal question?"

149

"You can ask but I'm not sure I'll give you an answer."

Alessandra chuckles and tosses her mane. "Do you have multiple orgasms?"

Where did that come from? I remember the shock of when it happened in Cap d'Antibes with Alexandre. "Do *you?*" I ask boomeranging her question.

"No. Never. And I never had an orgasm with a man. I wanted to…but…I tried…you know, but it just didn't happen."

"Well, that's nothing to be ashamed of. Lots of women go through that," I say carefully, not wanting to reveal anything too personal. "You know what? I'm going to grab that shower and then we can eat. I hope you like cold sesame noodles. There are puffed rice cakes, vegetable spring rolls and there's some spicy prawn curry as well."

"I'll heat up the oven."

"I won't be long."

I feel her eyes on my back as I saunter to the bathroom and she shouts after me, "Do you want to borrow a robe? Hey, Pearl, if you already checked out of your hotel, why don't you stay here tonight?"

I turn around. "No. Thank you for the offer but I can check into an airport hotel. I'm flying out at the squawk of dawn."

"As you please. Grab a terry-cloth robe from the bathroom. You know, you can chill out comfortably while we watch the movie. Have you seen *All About Eve?*"

"One of my favorite Bette Davis films - '*Fasten your seatbelts, it's going to be a bumpy night,*' " I say, quoting my favorite line.

"Oh dear, well, we can put on something else."

"No, that's perfect - I haven't seen it for years."

I shower and then we eat watching the movie. Eve

Harrington – what an insidious character - and Bette Davis's Margo Channing who's just turned forty. Oh, how I identify! Eve Harrington - a seemingly sweet-as-candy actress usurping her idol's position in such a scheming, clever way. The whole scenario reminds me of Sophie. The story is different but the intention is there: to slowly silently take over, to push out your rival with a smile on your face. Buying me my wedding gown, telling Alexandre she loves me, yet plotting behind my back. Yet she hasn't actually done anything *actively* bad so it looks as if I'm paranoid. Sure, she called me a 'cougar' and a 'stalker' a few months back but I shouldn't hold that against her forever. She did apologize, too. But I know she's up to no good.

So far, Sophie is winning. Getting her way with Alexandre - pushing me away from him.

We'll see if she succeeds.

Alessandra has been plying us both with champagne and because of the spiciness of the Thai food I've been glugging it down without really noticing. Uh oh, I have an early plane to catch and now I'm feeling woozy. But I'm so relaxed by the cozy log fire and she has a way of making me laugh with her ironic and direct sense of humor that I'm loathe to leave - just yet.

All About Eve ends and I'm sprawled out on the couch in Alessandra's terry-cloth robe, my hair still damp. She's gazing at me, her lips slightly parted.

"Pearl, this is our last ever moment together. Probably."

"Yes, it is. I don't think I'll be returning to LA."

She pouts. "Why?"

"It's too tough here. I mean, New Yorkers can be rough around the edges but at least what you see is what you get. Here things are subtly sinister – I can't explain it but I feel this place is a little Machiavellian - sugar-coated with a seductive sheen, which makes it all the more dangerous. Los Angeles is a magnetic place and you can get sucked in all too easily."

Alessandra temples her hands to her chin as if digesting my opinion and then says softly, "I sense you have a dark side to you, Pearl. And I think you need to be punished for being a little slutty in the past."

I stare at her in amazement. At first I want to slap her – what she has just said is way too close to the bone and I feel hurt - betrayed even. She's a woman, she should understand - know how tortured I am by my own guilt and self-blame about what happened to me. But then I'm overcome by...I can't even explain it...a sort of morbid intrigue. There is something fiendish and sinful about Alessandra and it draws me in.

She continues, "Before you leave this wicked town for good would you like to experience one last thrill?" She runs her fingers through her wavy hair. "You like living on the edge, don't you, Pearl? Experimenting? Today on the trapeze, for instance, and all those years ago putting yourself in danger with those horny, out-of-control footballers. What were you expecting? You knew it would end in tears, didn't you? You knew, yet you did it anyway."

My heart is pumping with both irritation and curiosity. I narrow my eyes. "Where's this leading?"

"Do you trust me?"

"Not really," I reply coolly.

"And that makes it all the more titilating, doesn't it? I know you want your fiancé to spank you, to flick a whip on your wet little pussy."

This woman is something else. What a nerve! I want to laugh out loud but what she's saying is secretly turning me on. The champagne has made me so relaxed that I feel fearless and a shiver of excitement shimmies through me. I tell her, "Like I said - Alexandre would never play S and M games with me even if I begged him. Anyway, I don't like being hurt."

She raises an eyebrow. "We would use a safe word."

I try to suppress a smirk. For some reason this conversation is amusing me although Alessandra has a dead-serious expression on her face. "*We?*" I ask.

"I'm going to blindfold you, Pearl. We can play a little fantasy game. You pretend in the darkness beneath your blindfold that I am Alexandre. See if you like it. If you don't then just shout out the word, *Sicily.*"

"Sicily?"

"You wanna choose something else?"

"You're serious about this, aren't you?"

"You need to purge your guilt about your past – extricate that feeling of culpability. I'm going to help you do that by punishing you. Then you'll be free. Call it witchcraft, think of it as a little spell, if you like."

As she says the word, 'spell' Lucifer jumps onto the couch and rubs his soft black fur against me. His tail brushes onto my slightly open robe and it touches my flesh seductively. He purrs loudly as if agreeing with his mistress.

"Pussy," she spits out.

Does she mean pussycat? Is she talking to Lucifer?

"You're a coward, Pearl," she clarifies.

"Alessandra, I'm not into being hurt. It's one thing reading about this kind of stuff in an erotic novel or seeing it in a film, but another doing it in real life. Okay, I admit, I'm curious but…"

She rolls her eyes. "Forget it. I thought it was a good idea – something to ease away your mental anguish – a way of striking out those bad dreams by administering a little light punishment - but if you're not into the idea…"

My mind is ticking over. Maybe she has a point. Perhaps this could be the answer - the champagne part of my brain thinks so, anyway. What harm is there in at least trying? This woman is slight, not as strong as I am - she can't hurt me. "Okay, Alessandra, but on one condition: no handcuffs. If I don't like it I want to be able to stop instantly."

"That's what the safe word is for."

"No restraints, I mean it. And only five minutes, just to see. No kissing. I'm not gay - kissing would be way too intimate."

She takes another swig of her champagne and grins wickedly – her full lips breaking into a smile that spreads across her whole face. "You're on."

She glides over to the other side of the room, her bare feet noiseless on the parquet floor. I watch her out of the corner of my eye. She stands on a chair and carefully brings down a long box from the top of a free-standing closet. She blows some dust off the top of it. A treasure trove, obviously unused for a long while. Or, more likely, Pandora's Box. Will evil things fly out when she opens it? My curiosity makes me sit up. *What am I doing?*

The lights are already dimmed and Alessandra lights several candles and some more rose incense. She puts on some music – Frank Sinatra's *Witchcraft* (how fitting) and sways her hips slowly to the rhythm. She's still in her jeans and I in her robe. Obviously, she wants to play Dom and have me as her Sub.

She's right, I'm a sucker for adventure. Most forty year-old women don't go rock climbing and swing from trapezes, let alone get engaged to a man fifteen years younger than they are. And most women, period, forty or not, do not decide to experiment with a dose of lesbian bondage. *Am I nuts?* My sensible side yells at me, 'yes' but my curiosity drives me on.

"Okay, Pearl," she whispers, her lilting Italian accent catching the R of Pearl, "lie flat on your back."

The L-shaped sofa is large and there's plenty of space for me to sprawl out. I do as she bids. The room is blissfully warm and I feel comfortable. The champagne has eased away the fury I felt for Alexandre earlier. I suddenly wonder - is this my way of getting back at him? Yes, he told me that he'd find it sexy for me to be messing about with another woman, but S and M? *I don't think so.*

I observe Alessandra open up her toy box and take out a whip. It has tassels at one end.

She stands over me and presses it up to my nose. "Smell this."

I sniff it in; it smells of perfume. She runs it gently about my face and the tassels tickle.

"Now let's get your dressing gown off. You won't be cold, will you?"

"No, it's lovely and warm here."

She helps me off with my robe and stands back as if admiring all of me. "You have a very sexy body, Pearl. I was looking at your ass earlier. So round and shapely, but not big. I bet that ass drives Alexandre wild."

"It does."

"Tell me what he likes to do to it."

I have my eyes closed now and I conjure up one of our last

love-making sessions before my mind went pear-shaped with nasty memories. "He likes licking me there along the crack, pinching my pussy lips at the same time and teasing my clit until I'm begging him to fuck me."

She bites her bottom lip. "Tell me more, it's making me horny."

"Sometimes he beats me with his cock. It's so big and always rock-hard – he slaps me with it on my ass and right up at my opening. Until I'm so wet I can't stand it anymore. Then he fucks me from behind until I come."

"D'you have anal sex?"

"No," I whisper. "He's never tried. He's very old-fashioned that way. He thinks men who do that must be secretly gay or something. Doesn't understand why anyone would do that to a woman."

"Very vanilla."

"Yes, very. But sex with him is incredible. Well, when I'm not having needle-dick visions of that horrible night, that is."

"That's what we're going to deal with now, Pearl. Beat away your guilt about that night with needle-dick and company."

Her accent makes me laugh. Not that the needle-dick thing is funny but it suddenly strikes me how ridiculous this whole scenario is. Both of us about to do this nutty experiment. I observe her graceful movements. She has now got a blindfold out of the box of tricks.

"Sit up a second, Pearl, let me put this on you."

I ease up from the couch realizing how floppy and relaxed I feel. I'm about to be whipped and I don't care. *This is madness!* She adjusts the black silk blindfold so I can't see a thing.

"Now lie back," she commands in her husky voice.

I lie back down. I can feel the tassels of the whip run up and down my flesh but surprisingly it's soft and soothing. She circles my breasts, not touching the nipple and guides it around my navel fluttering it about my Venus. I moan with pleasure.

"I can see you're getting wet, Pearl," she sing-songs, slapping me between the legs very slightly. But it doesn't hurt. "You're naughty, aren't you? Playing around with me behind your fiancé's back?"

"He wouldn't mind," I whisper, flexing my hips to meet the sweet brush of the tassels. But it's trailing back to my breasts now leaving my lower region bereft and needy for more. Then she stops and bends my knees up. I lie there in the darkness of my blindfold. I hear her getting something else out of the box.

"What are you doing?" I ask a little scared. Maybe this woman is crazy. People in Los Angeles have guns. She's a woman living alone in semi-countryside – she probably packs a pistol in that box of tricks. Uh, oh, am I about to have a snub-nose revolver held up to my head?

"Ssh," she says pressing her thumb against my lips, parting them and then grazing it along my front teeth. I lax my mouth. Being blindfolded is scary, but sexy.

Then I feel her hand on my wet slit and she's gently walking her fingers along my cleft and parting my lips down there. She doesn't touch my clit which is begging for attention, tingling with longing. She has something in her hands, what is it? Then I feel her slip something large inside me. I'm throbbing with pleasure. What is this she's putting inside my opening?

She tells me, "These are jiggle balls. Don't worry, they're new, never been used before. You can wear these all day – prescribed by gynecologists to strengthen the pelvic floor muscles but what I use them for is to make my pussy extra sensitive. Wear these about and by the time evening comes your orgasm is super intense."

I can feel the chilly metal slipping inside - alien but welcoming. I'm so wet they slide in with relative ease. I'm already feeling stimulated. Nice.

Her fingers are lightly stroking my clit now and I'm feeling double pleasure. She goes on, "They're called jiggle balls because they jiggle once inside – they contain weights so they vibrate gently when you move around. You know, you can go about your business, do your shopping, whatever, and nobody knows the little smirk you have on your face is because you've got a sexy little secret going on south of the border."

I moan quietly as Alessandra presses my clit deliciously.

She continues, "These balls stimulate your G spot for discreet arousal." She bursts out laughing. "Except, you know, Pearl, once I climaxed in the grocery store so it wasn't so discreet. I was feeling really horny and you know those big chest freezers they sometimes have? I'd had the balls inside me all day long so I was already pretty worked up and all I needed was a little nudge, you know? So I pressed my pussy up against the corner of it and had like, this mind-blowing orgasm right there in the store. Nobody saw me - supposedly - but I bet it got caught on camera. Some guy in a control room somewhere getting his rocks off, watching a video of me coming like crazy. These little silver balls work wonders. You can keep these when we're done. As a memento."

I'm lying back in a zone of sexual bliss. Jesus, this is sexy, I'm so aroused. She slides her finger inside me and circles it very, very slowly. The balls are warming up now – hot in fact from my burning Venus which is pulsating around them and clenching with anticipation. It's true, they're making me needy. She's got me, Alessandra has. I'm at her mercy – I need an orgasm. I'll do anything now to feel that release.

"Right, now I want you to sit up, turn over and get on your hands and knees doggy style. Stay on the couch."

"But this is so great, I'm so happy where I am just like this."

"Do as your told, you naughty girl. Up!" She taps the whip between my legs and it brings me to attention.

Still blindfolded, I crawl into the position she has described. I feel really vulnerable now – naked, my ass in the air. I sense the tassels tickling my opening as she guides the whip up and down.

"Get ready, slut!" and she brings the whip down on me. The tassels lash at my Venus lips. Ouch, it stings. Then I feel a soft stroking finger sooth my cleft. I'm clenching myself, I feel the balls inside me move – I'm still smarting from the sting. She's stroking my butt cheeks softly with her palm in circles and then, whack! She brings her hand down on me hard. I think it's her hand – it feels different. "That's for wanting too much cock at one time!" she warns.

I cry out, "That hurts!"

"So it should. But I'll be nice and kiss it better."

I feel her soft mane of hair tickling between my thighs and her lips are blowing at my opening now, her warm breath making me shimmer and pound in all the right places. She kisses me there. Oh God, oh yeah…I feel her tongue flickering at the back of me right at the base and move north towards my butt slit. Glad I had that shower and lathered sweet-smelling oils over my skin. She's running her tongue up and down and I'm bucking my hips at her – I can't help it. I'm teetering on the edge. Then there's a lull. Oh no, the punishment again? The trepidation is only making me all the hornier. *This is nuts! Why am I enjoying this?* Then I feel the whip thrash on my ass and then immediately tapping so softly against my clit as contact is made and then lost...trailing the whip softly from there up to the cleft of my butt...she does this over and over. The anticipation is killing me. My hips are gyrating - my Venus has morphed into a veritable humming V-8, buzzing with desire. My breathing is profound - I'm moaning, "Please Alessandra, please."

"Please what? You want me to whack you again?"

"Touch me, press it, make me come."

"Not so fast you bad girl who thinks cocks are the answer to her prayers." She slips what feels like her thumb into my wet slit and starts moving it around. The balls are doing their thing. I can feel the build-up...all she needs to do is stroke my clit...

But whack! Down comes the whip with the tassels. It really stings this time.

"That freaking hurt!" I have tears in my eyes.

"That's for getting gang raped, that's for putting yourself in so much danger. Tell me you won't do it again."

"Of course I won't, are you crazy?"

"I'm crazy about your sexy ass that makes me want to rub myself all over it and make my pussy come hard but I have a job to do and that's to make you never forget why I'm punishing you. To whip those filthy needle-dicks out of your memory." SLASH! The whip comes down on my ass again and I shriek this time. I must be sore as hell. "That's enough!" I yell at her. Should I scream *Sicily?*

"Tell me you'll kiss me first."

"That wasn't the deal, Alessandra!"

She pinches my pussy lips hard just at my entrance. The

smarting pain is mixed with desperate carnal lust as I feel myself about to come. But my clit is begging for just a nudge of pressure. I need that release so badly. Suddenly the idea of kissing her soft lips and licking her full, beautiful tits fills me with horny desire.

"Do what you did when we were in the bath and I'll come, please...I *will* kiss you Alessandra, I promise."

She trails the whip up along my stomach and on my nipples brushing the tassels over them. I groan with desire. She softly strokes my cleft with her hand and pressures my clit firmly with her whole palm with a few hard rubs. I rock back and forth to meet her hand. I feel a thunderous rush of blood well up and my orgasm bursts from deep inside. The silver balls, her palm, the image of her breasts, Alexandre's gorgeous, sexy face when he's fucking me - all unite into a wave of ecstasy. I push hard on her hand, the waves undulating through my core and I'm moaning, still blindfolded, all the sensations doubled by not being able to see.

My legs are trembling and I collapse face-down on the couch. I press my own hands between my legs to eek out the post-orgasm quavers. Like musical notes they are dancing through me, chiming and jingling, the balls heavy inside me, the tingling and shivers now light and feathery after feeling so deeply intense from within.

"Girl power," whispers Alessandra. "Tell me you liked that."

"I loved it," I murmur. "Well, not the beating bit but—"

"Stay there, I'm going to get some balm for that poor sexy ass of yours."

She goes off to the bathroom and comes back with some calamine lotion. I know because I recognize the smell. It reminds me of when my mother would rub it on me when I was a child after too much sun, which just makes the reality of what I've done hit home. *I am playing sex games with a lesbian!* Is it wrong? Now I've had my orgasm I regret saying what I did – I really don't want to kiss her - it's too intimate. I think of Julia Roberts in *Pretty Woman* and remember that's what her character said. I should go soon, anyway. Get out of here. I feel a wave of shame mixed with exhilaration. What a paradox!

I'm still lying on my front. Alessandra takes my wrists and ties them together with what feels like a bandana. *Why am I letting her do this?*

I say weakly, "I said, *no restraints*, Alessandra."

"Oh this is nothing. I just want to ensure you don't go trying to pleasure yourself. That's *my* job."

I chuckle. *I've just had an incredible orgasm, I don't need another!* "I'm good. My whole core has just exploded, believe me, Alessandra, I'm done. The last thing I need to do is pleasure myself."

"We'll see about that."

"What are you going to do now?"

She says nothing but begins to gently rub the lotion on my butt, careful not to hurt me. It's sore but not too bad. I'll live. But…oh God…here she goes again. Her massage is turning me on once more. *This is insane!* Her fingers gently open my cheeks and with a little pressure she rests her thumb at that sweet spot where my thighs join my ass – she's slipping her thumb inside me. Holy Moses – she's circling it now and those sexy jiggle balls are still there. Oh wow. Multiple orgasms are not something that happen often, not even with Alexandre…but…this…Holy Heaven.……this feels amazing.

162

Her thumb is inside, the balls are doing their thing – she's got her four fingers resting on my mound, on my clit...the pressure...oh wow....any second now I'm going to come again. I'm rubbing my Venus hard on her hand. This feels so horny. It's coming...it's coming...

But she stops.

What is she playing at?

My nails are clawing into the material of the couch, wrists in front of me tied with the silky bandana. She has me so worked up. Teetering on the edge. *Please!*

"Please Alessandra," I plead in a desperate voice.

"Quite a selfish lover, aren't you?"

But I told you I'm not gay. I don't do girls.

"Turn over," she commands.

I do as she says. I feel my wetness hot between my legs. I bring my arms down to touch myself. I just need that little push and...

"Not so fast." She grabs my wrists and puts my hands above my head. I'm on my back again. Ouch, my butt is sore. "Bend your knees up and press the small of your back into the couch, it'll take the pressure off your ass," she instructs.

I do as she says, all my nerve endings tingling with trepidation, my Venus pounding...wanting round two. Not round two of a beating...no, I think I'm done with that little experiment for good, but round two of....oh wow, I can feel her warm breath on my inner thighs. She splays my legs apart some more and I detect her mane of hair nestling between me. Softly. I flex my hips up higher to meet what I can feel is her tongue. Oh wow. She's licking me now with long swipes using just the tip of her tongue. I'm writhing and pressing my groin into her – her

163

tongue is resting so, so gently on my clit – I'm going to come, I'm going to come…

But she stops.

Pussy-teaser. "Please," I beg.

She's moved away from her position now. What's she doing? My blindfold is still keeping me in my dark little world, each movement is multiplied a hundred times – each sensation more pronounced. I smell the rose incense and calamine lotion and her sweet minty breath – she must have brushed her teeth in the bathroom. She's licking my tits now, flicking her tongue around my nipples, nibbling them gently with her teeth. I sense her hand on my head and she slips the blindfold off me in one quick movement. The room is dimmed but suddenly everything seems bright. Her cherry-red lips parted seductively, her dark hair falling like a cascade about her bare shoulders – she has taken off her shirt and her breasts are full, the nipples erect - but she's still got her jeans on, straddling me, not sitting on me, just kneeling on the couch. Tendrils of her long hair rest on my cheeks. She is breathtakingly beautiful and I gasp at this unusual situation of not just having an upcoming movie star desiring me and pleasing my desires but a *woman!*

"You really are stunning," I hear myself say.

Her lips graze me lightly on the chin and then linger on my mouth without moving. *I shouldn't do this!* But she smells so sweet, her skin soft as silk. I find myself parting my lips and offering her the tip of my tongue. Slowly – so slowly we lick each other, playing with just the tips, flickering together like a flame of a candle. Desire shoots like a current of electricity down to my groin. I moan into her mouth.

Her lips are lightly teasing - her finger tapping my clit as she kisses me. Oh, yeah. Her kiss gets deeper, more sensual and I think, *I am loving this.* She's making little circles now with her fingers flat against my mound, pressuring me in all the perfect places. I'm gyrating against her and yes, oh yes, the build, the stairway…I start climaxing in a rush of rapture – Seventh Heaven – ignoring any preconceived notions of what a woman should or shouldn't do with another female. My tied hands are grasping, fisting in her wild hair as she pleasures the fuck out of my Venus. I see stars of color flashing through my brain. The orgasm is long, it keeps going - rolling over me, under me, through me, the jingling balls wriggling about inside as I cry out with intense gratification.

Finally, the waves roll into ripples and the ripples begin to fade. Alessandra gets off the couch and adjusts her position. With one leg firmly on the floor and one still on the sofa she holds my knee and thrusts it between her crotch – the material of her jeans pressing hard into my knee. I feel her heat. All it takes is a few dry rubs and I see the expression on her face change to a clenching of the teeth, her nipples hard as nuts and with one last push she screams out. "I'm coming Pearl, coming hard."

This is a first! If Alessandra weren't so beautiful I would laugh out loud at the madness of it all but her vulnerable face as she looks at me with such an expression of bliss and her tight, peachy ass thrusting her crotch on my knee in such a sexy way as she tips herself into ecstasy, makes it all okay.

I Kissed a Girl and I Liked It. The song captures my imagination as the tune hums about in my head.

But Alessandra is looking serious. Like a guy who has just got what he wanted, she gets off me and slumps herself down into the armchair opposite. I'm relieved. The idea of post-coital cuddles with another woman would be going too far. It was curiosity. Sex. Carnal desire. A physical release. An adventure. But it's Alexandre I want, not a woman. That's clear to me. Crystal clear - however much fun I've just had.

I still stand by my resolution, though. I won't accept marriage if I have to live in a proverbial threesome with Sophie.

I observe Alessandra. She's lying back in the chair, her legs stretched out before her, her pretty toes pointed, her bare golden torso smooth as caramel.

"I have extremely intense orgasms, Pearl," she whispers. "Afterwards, I feel drained – wiped-out. This one's been building for a long time, thanks to you. Excuse me, I just feel like resting a while,"

I take the terry robe which has been strewn over the back of the couch and put it back on. "That's fine," I whisper back. I notice her eyes are closed now. Good. I can leave - slip away and she won't get upset. Phew.

I tiptoe to the bathroom, untie my wrists and gather my clothes together. I check out my butt in the mirror. It's red, alright, with a couple of obvious welts. Lucky Alexandre won't be around to see. I pull the jiggle balls out, wash them with hot soapy water and leave them by the sink – somehow I don't think I'll be using these again, fun as they were. I get dressed back into my panties and jeans, gently easing each article of clothing over my sore behind, trying not to graze the sensitive skin. I quickly put my bra and T-shirt back on. My sweater must be in the kitchen.

I tiptoe past her. "Bye," I say quietly but she doesn't hear me. Or she's pretending not to. What a fascinating character. It seemed like it was her mission to kiss me and now she got what she wanted she feels as if she's won me in some way. But I won't be returning.

I grab my sweater and handbag from the kitchen. I check inside for my car keys, but now I remember…I didn't put them there because they always get lost in an ocean of darkness. Where did I leave them? By the stove? In a bowl? Where? Lucifer trots into the kitchen, light on his paws, and starts doing a pole dance against the furniture and my legs.

"Where did I put my keys, Lucifer?" I whisper. I don't want to wake Alessandra, I need to hightail it out of the scene of the crime – yes, I do feel as if I've broken the law. CSI could be arriving any minute to scan for evidence. I am a naughty girl, no two ways about it.

As if by magic, Lucifer jumps up onto one of the countertops and starts clawing at another basket piled high with bills. "You clever puss," I marvel, finding the BMW rental keys right there. "Are you a warlock pussycat? Do you understand human talk?"

He meows as if answering and stares at me with his shimmering green eyes. *Jesus, this cat really is magic!* I grab the keys from the basket and then something catches my eye. Again! But this time it isn't a letter. It's a photo peeking out from under a bill. I freeze. Is it really…? No, surely not. My hearts starts pounding. I ease it out from the pile.

Alessandra…and yes, unmistakably…Sophie. Nude bodies entwined in an intimate embrace, Sophie's hand on Alessandra's breast - both grinning away at the camera. The picture tells a story…best friends? Nuh, uh - I don't think so. They look like a couple in love.

I grab the photo and shove it in my purse.

And run.

11

I drive the car over the creek very carefully as frogs have gathered for their night time chit-chat and I don't want to run any over. The noise is impressive as they croak in the pebbled rush of water amongst the bulrushes. Once I am safely out of sight from Alessandra's lair, I pull the car over at the end of the potholed driveway, kill the engine and turn on my cell which has been switched off for hours.

There are six voicemail messages. I listen to the first.

"Pearl darling, we got cut off. As I said, I'm on my way to LA. I've organized a plane. Can you meet me at the Van Nuys Airport in…I don't know, five hours or so?"

No mention of Sophie. As if he hadn't heard a word I said.

Next voicemail: "Pearl, chérie, why aren't you picking up? I'm about to take off. I'm gutted about what you told me. Hang on in there. We'll talk about all this when I see you. It was not your fault, baby. We all have a past. It's nothing to be ashamed of.

And don't think I won't hunt those fuck-heads down for what they did to you. But first we have our marriage to attend to. I've organized it all and we're going to Vegas tonight. Meet me at the Van Nuys Airport and I'll pick you up there. The pilot will wait and we'll fly to Las Vegas."

Again, nothing about Sophie or separating the business. *This guy has not heard me.* He thinks we can just marry and that will be that - everything sorted, solution over! *No, Alexandre, I will not just marry you in Vegas before you've dealt with HookedUp first! Especially now that I know Sophie has been screwing with me and my movie deal right from the beginning – she is Alessandra's LOVER! A coincidence – I don't think so!*

Next voicemail – sent five hours later. "Landed, baby. Your cell is still switched off, what the fuck is going on? I'm really worried now."

Finally, the penny is dropping.

Next voicemail: "Okay, baby, I get it; you're really pissed off about Sophie. I swear I'll deal with it but please, please trust me on this. I just want us to get married. We'll be a team and we can sort it out together. Where are you? I've hired a car, I'm on my way to the hotel in Santa Monica."

Next voicemail. His voice sounds as if he's almost in tears. "Baby, they say you checked out. I'm so worried, you alone in LA and stuff. The only thing I can think of, right now, is that you're at Alessandra's. But she's not picking up her phone, either. I'm on my way there now. Please don't leave. Please, Pearl. I beg you. I need you. I'm coming to find you."

Next voicemail…hang on, this isn't him. A woman's voice. An English accent. Educated, softly-spoken. "Pearl, you don't know me. I'm sorry to bother you like this. I finally tracked down your number. My name is Laura. Alexandre's ex...maybe you know who I am?"

My heart is pounding through my sweater, my hands burst with a sheen of sweat - a prickly nausea envelops my entire body. Why I feel so nervous I'm not sure...a premonition?

The urgent but friendly voice goes on: "I'm calling to warn you. Sophie is really crazy. She could be out to hurt you. I'm sorry but...." There's a long pause.... "I had a terrible accident several years ago and could have died. It wasn't an accident at all. Sophie tried to kill me."

I press my ear closer to my phone. There's a slight pause and the voice continues:

"Why do you think I broke up with Alexandre? I had to keep well away. Stay away from her, too, Pearl. I know you love Alexandre but your life is at stake. She's powerful. She's even more dangerous now than then. She knows people...she could have you topped off at the click of her fingers. *Do not go to Vegas.* It's too dangerous for you there. She owns great chunks of it... hotels et cetera, corrupt police officers, officials all in her pocket like little pawns doing whatever she asks. Sophie could do anything and will, believe me. I won't bother you again but as one woman to another, I thought I owed you this. Goodbye, Pearl. Good luck."

I feel sick - all this information flooding into my exhausted brain like sewerage. *Sophie tried to kill Laura?* Then why does Laura still go to Alexandre's house in Provence with her husband for vacations knowing she might bump into Sophie? Alexandre told me they were friends and that Sophie thought 'the sun shone out of Laura's ass.' Unless...he was lying, sticking up for his sister, as usual. Painting her with a rose-tinted brush when in fact, Sophie still hates Laura. *Jesus – she tried to murder her?* That nutcase will stop at nothing!

And that's just the tip of the iceberg. Sophie and Alessandra are a *couple?????* Or if not a couple, best friends/lesbian fuck buddies. Alessandra lied to me, pretended she'd only ever spoken to Sophie, that she didn't know her personally. *I was totally set up by Sophie. It was all planned out!* Alessandra Demarr was suggested for the movie role by Sam Myers. Meanwhile, Sam Myers was in cahoots with Sophie from word go. Clever. Really clever. Knowing I wanted a female lead for the role, Samuel Myers put the idea of Alessandra Demarr into my head – made it look like it was my choice all along. Or *was* it my choice? Now I can't even remember our conversation.

Alessandra and Sophie lovers? But Sophie's married! She has a step-daughter. Alexandre never mentioned anything about his sister being *gay*.

Never before have I felt such a fool. So dumb. Summa cum laude? They got that wrong, alright. What a dense dumbass I've been, congratulating myself on getting a gay female lead who is not only Sophie's lover but who also seduced me! No, *worse!* She didn't even have to seduce me – I was up for it. Like putty in her hands. Acting like a little slut again.

I got snagged right into Sophie's spider web. Tangled right in the middle of her Black Widow trap.

Laura's right, Vegas would be suicide.

I put the car into drive and move off. Great, I told Alessandra where I was going. Sophie could have me tracked down in Kauai. But I guess Sophie would find me anywhere in the world – she has the means and with GPS as sophisticated as it is nowadays hunting me down would be a piece of cake if she set her mind to it. She wants me to back off from Alexandre. And I want *her* to back off. Who is going to win this duel?

It depends on him. Who does he love more? His own flesh and blood? Or me? He once told me that the expression, *blood is thicker than water* doesn't exist in the French language. If so, he'd better prove it.

As I'm moving off, a car is pulling into Alessandra's driveway but I can't see the face of the person behind the wheel. Alexandre? Jesus, maybe it's Sophie. Either way, I rev my engine and double my speed. I look in my rear-view mirror and think the driver hasn't seen me, but I'm wrong. The car is screeching in a U-turn and coming right after me. I hang a sharp left on PCH in the direction of LAX, just getting the green light in time and flatten my foot on the accelerator. If it's Sophie, I need to outrun her. Alexandre, ditto. I know him – he's so persuasive he'll have me on that plane, abducting me and whisking me off to Vegas to tie the knot. He's used to getting what he wants.

Well not this time, buddy.

My foot is all the way down. I'm cruising fast. This BMW is smooth and speedy – thank God I traded in the Cadillac. I'm outrunning the driver, way ahead but can see its headlights flashing at me. I feel as if I'm in some car chase in a movie and it gives me a wicked thrill as a surge of adrenaline spikes my veins. The driver is careering about corners with a keen, formula one style. Uh, oh, I recognize that technique – that easy panache, those gear changes. I see what kind of car it is – a sleek, black Mercedes – yes, that's him, that's Alexandre. I don't stand a chance. We are both hell bent for leather, flying two times past the speed limit as if we were on a German autobahn. We'll both be arrested, for sure. He's catching up with me now, zooming between two other cars. He has overtaken me and I can't do a U-turn.

I'm busted. If I don't want us both killed I'd better pull over. I see a safe spot up ahead and pull into a restaurant parking lot. He does the same a little way ahead. My heart's pounding but I'm secretly enjoying the attention. A twenty-five year-old sex-god, babe-magnet, the best looking man in the Universe is tracking me down and wants to take me to Vegas to marry him! Hello? *Am I dreaming?* He's running towards my car now and I can't help it; a huge grin is spread right across my face. I zap down my window, trying so hard to stifle my beaming smile, biting the insides of my cheeks. But he's got my number.

He leans into the open window of my car. "Quite a madwoman, aren't you? Trying to get us both killed?"

"I meant what I said, Alexandre," I say, pursing my lips to stop myself laughing, my only ammunition against his drop-dead gorgeous smile – a smile that's giving me butterflies and turning my stomach inside-out. "I'm not going to Vegas with you; I'm going to visit my father in Kauai."

He opens my door and leans in, his apple-mint breath on my face. He says in a soft, low voice, his face touching mine, "Correction. *We* are going to Vegas. Now. I'm going to marry you tonight or," he looks at his watch, "early tomorrow morning as it's already ten-thirty. "Then *we* are going to Kauai for our honeymoon."

"NO!" I shout. But it's too late. He grabs the keys out of the ignition and scoops me out of the driver's seat and hauls me over his shoulders as if I'm a weightless doll. He walks round to the trunk.

I'm kicking and flailing about. "Put me down Alexandre!"

"No. You're acting like a child, Pearl, and need to be treated like a child." He opens the trunk and takes out my suitcase - awkward but he manages. His determination and strength have him holding the suitcase in one hand and the other clamped about my rear in a tight vice. He locks the car with the remote. He's marching forward now towards his rental car, his arm still clenched around me. Ouch, my sore, whipped butt hurts! I can't escape, he has me in a firm hold. The fireman's lift. Oh yes, he knows I love this fireman thing, however much I'm screaming and kicking.

"Let me down!" I cry, pummeling his back with my fists.

"No, Pearl. Stop behaving like a wayward teenager. You're coming with me. I'm fed up with this nonsense."

"I'm not marrying you, Alexandre Chevalier! Not until you sort—"

"Stop telling me what to do," he barks, his gait strong as he strides towards his car. "You're marrying me and that's the end of it."

I suddenly think of something. "You can't marry me, you don't have my divorce papers. So there!"

"Oh no? I've had Suresh get them couriered over to the hotel we're saying at in Vegas. All will be quite legal, I can assure you."

We arrive at his car. With one hand he opens the trunk, chucks my case in and, keeping a tight grip on me with the other arm so I can't escape, lowers me into the back seat and lays me inside as if I were a child not allowed in the front seat with her daddy. Then he locks the door. I try to open it from inside but it won't let me out. Child safety locks, no doubt. I pound on the windows.

He comes around to his side, opens his door and jumps in.

"Not so fast, Pearl Robinson, soon to be Pearl Chevalier. You are *not* running out on me. You did that once in France and I won't let it happen again." He starts the engine, puts it into first and revs forward, Formula One Style.

"So I'm your prisoner?"

"Yes. And then you'll be my wife."

"Also in jail. Do not pass GO - DO NOT COLLECT $200."

"There'll be more than $200 to collect, of that you can be quite sure."

"But still in jail."

"Yes." He smiles and adds, "A very pretty, gilded jail where you can have anything you want."

"Except my freedom."

"Believe me, you'll be there of your own free will."

"Like now? Trapped in the back of this Mercedes being abducted into marriage?"

A gentle smirk edges his curvy, dark red lips. "I know what's best for you, Pearl. Trust me. You need to marry me."

The arrogance! I would laugh but it's not funny. I'm crying now, tears trailing down my cheeks. "You're taking me to my death."

He laughs out loud and changes smoothly into fourth.

"I'm not kidding, Alexandre. Laura called. She says Sophie tried to kill her."

"Nonsense."

"She did! She says it was no accident and that Sophie owns chunks of Vegas and will have me murdered."

He doesn't say anything. Just keeps his eyes on the road.

"What is *wrong* with you? You sister is insane and you're too blind to see it!"

"I agree, my sister is a little eccentric, shall we say, but she's not going to try and have you killed."

"How do you *know*?"

"Because I know her. I know how her mind works."

"Like she stabbed your father in the groin? She is *dangerous*."

He turns his head abruptly to me. His lips close tightly, bitterly – his eyes flash with rage. "He deserved what he had coming to him. Don't you *dare* defend that vicious monster."

"It doesn't let Sophie off the hook. She's out to get me."

"She's jealous, Pearl, that's all. She'll get used to you."

"She will *not* get 'used to me' because I'm bailing, Alexandre. I value my life too highly, however much I love you. I'm not going to marry you with your whack-job sister in the picture."

"I made some calls tonight. I'm selling her my share of HookedUp. Once and for all. Satisfied? Most men wouldn't let their girlfriends pussy-whip them the way you have with me about this, but because American women have a history of dominating their men, I'll forgive you. But just this once. It won't happen again, Pearl. This is the last time you tell me what to do. Do you understand." *No question mark but a statement.*

I am speechless. Pussy-whipped? I don't know whether to laugh or cry. Instead I blurt out, "I got pussy-whipped tonight. Literally."

He looks around at me with a wry smile and then back at the road. "Oh yes?"

"Yes, A bit of lesbian S and M." *There, said it.* "Surely you don't want to marry a quasi lesbian who got beaten by your sister's lover? Oh, and by the way, thanks for letting me in on the fact that Sophie is gay. Another secret you've been hiding from me."

"I didn't think it was my place to reveal Sophie's sexual

preferences. It's something we never discuss – she's very private. It was up to her to tell you. What do you mean, 'my sister's lover?' "

"What?? So it's true then, she's gay?"

"Yes, she's gay. She kept it quiet from me for years but I always had my suspicions. What do you mean, 'my sister's lover?' Are you talking about Alessandra Demarr?"

"Yes, I found a photo which I stole for evidence as I'm fed up with you telling me I'm imagining things. They are lovers. At least that's what the photo is spelling out loud and clear."

He changes the music. *Leaving on a Jet Plane*. How apt. "Interesting," he mumbles.

"What?? Why do you not seem shocked by this?"

"Sophie must have got together with her when we went backstage that time at the theatre - when we saw her in that play."

"What? Alexandre, why didn't you tell me this?"

"I did. I told you we saw a play of hers in London. Sophie wanted to congratulate her so we went to the green room backstage afterwards, but I got bored waiting so I left. Sophie stayed, though. She never told me the two of them had anything going on, or that they'd even met. I had no idea. And you had a little fun with Alessandra, too? Oh well…keep it in the family." He laughs.

"Stop it!" I yell leaning forward, still riding in the back seat. "I am *disgusted!* I feel used and dumb and a total freaking idiot. Why did I not see this? She seduced me, Alexandre, *and I let her.* My ass is so sore I can hardly sit. She whipped me, she made me come, she…she…" I find myself wailing through angry, shameful tears.

He turns the music down. "Ssh, now chérie, it's so not important in the great scheme of things." But he still has a slight smile on his face as if the whole thing tickles him somehow.

"Why the hell do you want me anyway?" I sniffle. "I had a threesome with two guys that went all wrong. I'm a quasi lesbian. I can't do a work deal without being totally screwed over. I can't look a penis in the eye, excuse the pun...I'm a basket-case. I am a disaster. This is all wrong, Alexandre, this is all screwed-up. *I* am screwed up. Really, I'm not the person you thought I was. I'm not Miss Sweetie-Pie, Star-Spangled American Cutie, Golden Girl. Look at me, I'm all over the place."

He changes gear again. "I know."

"No, you don't *know!* You thought I was perfect."

He threads his arm to the back seat and holds onto my hand. "Perfect for me, chérie. You think I want Miss Goodie-Two-Shoes? That I could relate to someone like that with my fucked-up past? I know who you are, Pearl, maybe even better than you know yourself. You're a contradiction, a paradox, a mix of all things messy and delightful. We've only known each other four and a half months but you are my *media naranja* – my soul mate - I knew that the second I laid eyes on you."

"The other half of the orange?" I snivel, grabbing some Kleenex from my purse and blowing my runny nose. "That Spanish expression you wrote me in your love letter?"

"That's right. We fit perfectly together. We're two separate orange halves that make up one whole."

I exhale with frustration but climb forward and maneuver myself into the passenger seat so we can have a more normal conversation. All Alexandre's love and forgiveness still doesn't solve the Sophie problem. This is exasperating. I feel as if I have been left to bubble and boil in Sophie and Alessandra's witches' cauldron. With Lucifer purring away, observing the whole crazy scene.

"Well, this is all a big shock for me, I can tell you," I say buckling up, remembering Bette Davis's line in *All About Eve*, 'Fasten your seatbelt, we're in for a bumpy night.' "I mean finding out about Sophie being gay, being Alessandra's girlfriend and, oh yes, P.S. Sophie is married."

"So? You think she's the first gay person to be married? It helps her social status, not to mention fiscal benefits. In France, being single's expensive. It's way more cost-effective to have a spouse."

I glare at him. "Is that why you want to marry me, to save on tax?"

"I file in America, chérie. My primary residence is New York, in case you haven't noticed. And no, I would never marry for financial reasons, you know that. Sophie's different – she's obsessed with money, as you are well aware."

"I feel grossed out. I might as well have had sex with Sophie herself. I kissed Alessandra. I let her whip me!"

He looks at me for a second, still vaguely amused. "And are you over it now? Cured of your bondage curiosity? Because don't ask *me* to get the handcuffs out and spank you."

I shuffle in my seat trying to find a comfortable position that doesn't chafe my tender butt. "Yes, I'm over it. It hurts. No more, thank you very much, my derrière is really sore."

His lips curve very slightly. "Good. Now can we get on with our relationship or do you have some more sniffing about to do?"

"Are you pissed at me?"

"What I had envisioned in my obviously very boring male imagination was a little kissing between two beautiful women, some light sexual entertainment, not my fiancée being beaten with a whip by my sister's lover."

"Yeah, well, I regret it now, that's for sure."

I suddenly remember all the dirty details that Alessandra shared with me about her 'ex' liking hairy underarms. The 'ex' obviously being Sophie, the 'tigress in bed.'

"It was an experiment," I say, excusing myself. "I wanted to beat out those nasty memories of that fateful night – wipe out my past."

Alexandre takes in a deep breath as if to say, *Good luck*.

"What, you think that's crazy?"

"Revenge is a dish best served cold," he replies ominously.

"What are you trying to say, Alexandre - what are you telling me?"

"Nothing, just quoting a rather fitting line from Shakespeare – or maybe not Shakespeare at all; perhaps it's some old Sicilian proverb."

Sicily. Alessandra. Yes, come to think of it I've heard that expression in *The Godfather* – Michael Corleone talking about how his father gave him that very same advice – *Revenge is a dish that tastes best when served cold*. I remember what Alexandre said to me on the phone earlier about the footballers - that he'd 'track those fuck-heads down' - and then I wonder, is that what he did with his father - serve him up a cold dish of revenge years later? His father's 'disappearance' – a cold payback dish that Alexandre took out of the freezer, thawed and served up when his dad was least expecting it? I'm dying to ask but every time I mention his father he gets riled. Now is not the moment to press him.

The car breaks smoothly to a halt. I can see the private jets clustered together a way off – Van Nuys Airport isn't a maze like

LAX. "We've arrived," Alexandre lets me know in a serious voice.

"I'm not going to Vegas."

"Yes you are."

"I'm not getting out of this car."

He laughs. "Do you want me to carry you in a fireman's lift again?"

"I'll scream and attract attention so you'll let me go."

"Not a chance. I'm keeping a firm grip on you until you've got that ring on your finger. I'll gag you if I have to. You want a bit of rough play, a bit of bondage? – you've got it, baby."

"What good will a dead wife be to you?" I shout. "Sophie will have me 'topped off' as Laura put it. Yes, that was the expression she used."

"Laura and Sophie get on fine – this is all ridiculous, I can't believe Laura called you and said that."

I fumble in my handbag for my cell. "Right, if you don't believe me, I'll play you the message!" I squeal.

He pretends he hasn't heard. "Where shall we go for our honeymoon? Anywhere in the world – you name it, baby, we can go. Kauai or Bora Bora. We can leave straight after the ink is dry on our marriage certificate if you don't fancy hanging about Vegas."

I want to scream. *Why is he ignoring me?* I grapple about for my phone in my oversize bag. *Where is it?* "Alexandre, why are you not listening? Your nutcase sister is going to kill me and all you're doing is laughing and in total and utter denial! She tried to kill Laura! Where is my goddam phone?"

"Calm down, Pearl."

I try to unlock my car door again but he grabs my wrists. I

stamp my legs on the floor. "I will NOT calm down!" Then I fish about in my bag again and finally locate my cell. Suddenly, a brilliant idea flashes into my brain like a torchlight. I take a deep breath and say. "Okay, fine, Alexandre. I'm coming along. I'll be quiet and behave but please keep an eye on me until we have gotten the hell out of Vegas. I'm scared."

"Good girl. And don't worry, I won't let you out of my sight. Ready now?"

"I think my cell fell out of the side pocket of my handbag," I lie.

"What a bummer, there's nothing worse than losing your phone. I'll buy you another. That one was outdated anyway."

"Never mind," I grumble.

He gets out of his side and quickly dashes around to open my door. I generally love that about Alexandre; he has such gentlemanly manners; always treats me with such respect, opening doors for me – except for *now*, throwing me over his shoulder like I'm a little girl – ignoring my plea. He's so dominating it worries me. Do I want to marry this man? As things stand at the moment, no, I don't. I can just see myself lying dead in a ditch somewhere in the suburbs of Vegas or in a dumpster with a bullet through my brain, or covered in liquid cement like some Jane Doe in a CSI Las Vegas episode. Alexandre admitted Sophie was 'eccentric' but he still won't stop her mad games And now he's putting my life in danger! I glare at him furiously.

He helps me out of the car and puts both his hands about my waist. "Christ, you're beautiful," he murmurs with hooded sex-eyes, raking me up and down as if he wants to eat me alive.

"Thank you," I mumble, bowing my head to stop his burning

gaze - loathing him and loving him simultaneously.

"C'est normal," he says in French and then takes my face in his large hands tilting my chin up and planting a firm kiss on my mouth. My heart is racing. His devastating good looks, his flashing green eyes, his soft, dark red lips…but more than all that, the adrenaline rush of what I'm about to do…

I break the kiss. "I really need to go to the bathroom."

"You can go when you're on the plane."

"Don't we need to go through some sort of security though?"

"Lately they've got a little picky – sometimes they frisk you with the metal detector thing before you board."

"That's what I was afraid of," I say, thinking I have metal balls inside me jiggling away. But then I remember that I took them out.

He smiles wryly. "Why, have you got a pistol on you?"

"No, just…well, I've got my period. I would really like to use the bathroom now before we board."

"You're just saying that. You'll try to do a runner."

"That's one of those British expressions you picked up from Laura, isn't it?"

"I have a feeling you'll try and slip away, Pearl."

"Don't be silly," I assure him, holding his hand and leading him to the building where some double doors are. "I just want to freshen up a bit and those airplane toilets are so squished – even on private jets - you can hardly turn around. Anyway, we have to drop the rental car keys off, don't we?"

"All I have to do is make a call and someone will come and pick up the keys."

"But I need to use the bathroom to clean up."

"Alright, but don't dawdle. This is already taking far too

long."

We find the ladies room.

"Why don't you drop off the car keys while I go to the toilet?" I ask, knowing he'll say no.

"Some chance. I'll wait here."

Alexandre hovers outside the door watching me suspiciously as I go in. I rush inside to have a scout about. No windows.

I come out again grimacing. "It stinks in there - half the toilets are blocked up. I need to find another."

"Come on, this is ridiculous, just go on the plane."

"I have blood all *over* me," I hiss at him.

I march ahead, desperate to bring my plan to fruition but it looks as if I'll be getting on that jet, like it or not. I find a new bathroom and do a quick check over. Bingo, there's a tiny window high up. I go over and see if I can open it. Just. It'll be a real squeeze but I'll try. I search in my bag and get out what I need. All my cash and my passport. I stuff it in my jeans' pockets. I casually come out of the ladies room. Alexandre is standing there, legs astride in his Alpha male stance, watching my every movement. I smile nonchalantly.

I edge up close to him, fingering the expensive material of his sharp, charcoal-grey suit jacket. "You look so handsome. How come you're wearing a suit today?"

He strokes the knuckles of my hand. "I didn't get a chance to change. I double-backed on that meeting in Montreal, remember? Chasing about after you, Ms. Pearl Robinson. But not for much longer though," he glances at his watch, "before I make you mine. You won't be Robinson any more. *Pearl...*" he says, rolling his tongue around the R of Pearl... "*Chevalier.* Sounds good, doesn't it?"

"Can't wait," I answer sweetly. "Hold my handbag, will you? There aren't any hooks on the back of the doors in there. Disgusting, I hate putting my handbag on the floor with all those germs everywhere." I give him my bag and hug him closely, slipping my hand surreptitiously into his jacket pocket until I find what I need. I distract him meanwhile with a kiss, gliding my teasing tongue along his lower lip and then I nip him there with my teeth. I lock my eyes with his. "I love you, Alexandre Chevalier, whatever happens, remember that. You'd better call the pilot and tell them we're on our way. I'll be a while in there, though. I need to change my panties." I hold a 'fresh pair' up at him (which is, in reality, a bunch of Kleenex scrunched in my hand with his car keys inside) …but it does the trick.

"I'll wait over there," he says, awkwardly handling my bag, as if it were a bomb. Why is it men find a woman's handbag so embarrassing? But he seems relaxed now, getting out his cell phone as he makes a call.

I race into the ladies room making a dash to the window. I climb on the toilet seat trying not to make any noise and raise my leg up, twisting and contorting myself into yogi-like positions until I am able to squeeze myself through the window. Better this than dead in Vegas, I think. It's dark out there and it's hard to tell where I'm going to land. All I have is the wad of dollar bills in my front jeans' pocket with the car key, my passport in the back pocket. My cell and everything else is in my handbag with him. There's no point bringing any of it - he could trace the movement on my credit cards and cell phone - and would. My heart's pounding in my chest. I'm falling head-first, now, and manage to twist my torso back around so I land on my feet the other side. My eyes dart about to fix my location. Luckily, this airport is fairly small and I spot the position where we parked the Mercedes. I sprint like crazy until I reach it.

I leap inside, turn on the ignition and drive like a bat out of hell.

12

Anthony's apartment is up on a hill in a beautiful tree-lined street in Pacific Heights. He and Bruce live in part of a stately Edwardian house which has been divided into three condos. His is the first floor sporting huge bay windows that look out over the city of San Francisco. It is light and roomy, decorated impeccably with graceful feminine furniture and walls painted in robin's-egg blue and whites that are not white but tinged with subtle tints of ivory - worthy of a spread in a designer magazine. There are two large fireplaces and detailed crowned moldings that run around the ceiling. Dead centre, an elegant crystal chandelier hangs like dripping jewels – a 'souvenir' that he and Bruce brought back from Venice, Italy. Which is where my eyes are fixed now, as I lie on the sofa in the living room contemplating what I should do next. It's nine a.m. - the morning after the night before, and I still haven't gone to bed yet.

Bruce, thank God, is visiting his parents in Napa Valley so I don't have to make small talk with him. I am not in the mood to make an effort with my brother's other half and am exhausted from last night's long drive. I look like hell, too.

I drove without stopping. At every moment I half expected to hear a helicopter above me searching with headlights for a Ms. Pearl Robinson, 'belonging to' a certain, Mr. Alexandre Chevalier. But I made it through the night. I guessed he would have suspected that I got on a plane to Kauai. Sorry, Dad, next time. Besides, Sophie will be expecting me to be there and I'm too freaked out to risk it – I want to stay out of her radar. Alexandre has called here, of course, but Anthony did a great job of sounding shocked and worried. I feel terrible, thick with guilt but what else can I do? Anthony seems to be enjoying all the drama but thinks I'm nuts not to have snapped up the wedding opportunity in Vegas. That's what he says but his ironic sense of humor can have you easily fooled sometimes.

Anthony minces into the living room in his pink silk pajamas. I am still in a trance, staring at that flickering crystal chandelier which is catching beams of morning light flooding through the bay windows. He brings in two large mugs of steaming drinks – coffee for himself and cocoa for me.

He sets the mugs on the coffee table on top of a thick book about Renaissance Art. "Just hire a bodyguard, Pearly. Get the marriage over and done with," he says carrying on with this morning's no-sleep conversation. I still haven't got any shut-eye at all.

I cover my yawning mouth. "Dead in a dumpster somewhere with a ring on my finger? What good would that do?"

"As long as I'm your next of kin and can inherit half of

Alexandre's empire," he jokes.

I glare at him.

"Seriously, Pearl, he's behaving like a total, control-freak asshole. Of course you can't go through with this union as things are right now. He can't just *abduct* you into marriage, that's insane. Even I get that."

"Yes, well, he's a man who's used to getting what he wants."

"To me it screams insecurity. A man who is so hooked-up on you, HookedUp, pardon the pun – so obsessed with you that it's scary. Like you're his possession. It won't be long before he arrives here, or sends someone – I could tell by his voice on the phone that he didn't quite believe me when I said you weren't here. There's probably someone watching the front door as we speak, waiting to pounce on you. Lucky the rental car is parked in the underground parking, anyway. I'll warn the neighbors not to say a word."

"He'll think I've gone to Hawaii."

"Nuh, uh, he's already checked all the flights out of LA and has people on the case. He said so on the phone."

I sigh. "I feel mean and guilty. I should call and tell him where I am."

"I bet he already knows where you are."

"How?"

"He has a whole team of private detectives working around the clock – that's what he told me, or warned me, more like. If you stay here he'll be on the front doorstep any minute now throwing you over his shoulder again and riding off into the sunset with you on his galloping black stallion."

"You make it sound so romantic."

"Well, it is romantic, in a way. Who wouldn't dream of a guy so in love with you that he's willing to take you hostage? Especially one as drop-dead gorgeous as Alexandre. However, this psycho sister shit is no joke and I totally see, Pearly, where you're coming from."

"You do?"

"Yes, she sounds like a total fruitcake. And a dangerous one at that."

"But he just doesn't *get* it. He refuses to take it seriously, just tells me that she'll 'get used to me'. The fact that she wheedled her way into Samuel Myers and my movie deal doesn't faze him at all. Alexandre acted like I was over-reacting and P.S. he forgot to let me in on the fact that he knew about it."

"It sounds as if he and Sophie are so close after what happened when he was a child that no matter *what* she does he will always forgive her and make excuses for her until the day he dies. Blood is thicker than water, and I'm sorry, Pearl, but you are the water and she is the blood. He's obviously crazy about you but he wants to have his cake and eat it too. He wants you both in his life and is juggling everything to keep it so."

"Yeah, well, I won't be in his life much longer if she has her evil way – I'll be dead."

"You really believe she could try and *kill* you?"

"I told you, Laura called to warn me. She sounded really kind. Really concerned. She supposedly tripped down some stairs because the next door neighbor's child had left some toys there. But she ended up in a wheelchair because of it – she could have *died*. The whole scenario sounds suspicious to me."

"She's still in a wheelchair?"

"No, apparently she's all better now. Just has a vague limp. But it was a miracle that she was able to walk again. Poor thing."

"What's she like?"

"Very nice, I think – does a bunch of stuff for disabled charities. Despite what happened, she hasn't felt sorry for herself in any way. From photos she looks like a super-model. Legs that reach up to her armpits, about five foot ten tall, a body to die for, a face like an angel, long blonde hair and sporty. At least she *was* sporty once before the 'accident' – I think she's doing round the clock physical therapy and is doing really well. Alexandre mentioned that she wants to sail again. To compete - so she's dedicated to getting a hundred percent better. So brave. She sounds like a really admirable person."

"They're still in contact?"

"Yes, they're still friends. He still cares for her."

"Does that make you jealous?"

"It would but she's happily married with a husband who dotes on her. Her childhood sweetheart who she knew before she met Alexandre. Of course, that pang of envy is there, knowing how in love Alexandre was with her once and, as I said, she really is beautiful but you know, it was a long time ago."

Anthony takes my hand in his and says softly, "*You're* beautiful, Pearl."

I look at him in shock. "That's the nicest thing you've said to me for years."

"I know. I'm sorry. I owe you a big apology. I've been a total ass for so long. I'm *really* sorry, sis, I guess I must have been envious of you and holding in a lot of anger about John."

"Envious? Of *me?*"

"I always felt that Mom loved you more. She always confided in you, not me, especially towards the end. It made me resentful inside and I blamed you for all sorts of things. I now realize I was

191

wrong. Will you ever forgive me?"

My eyes are prickling with tears and I feel a lump in my throat. "Thank you, Anthony for that. It means the world." I hug him, his bear-like body is now trembling as his tears come gushing out. "Pearly, I feel like such a big, fat failure. When Bruce nearly died it knocked the wind out of me. I thought I was going to be alone forever and it was then I stopped and thought about you. Really took responsibility for the way I've been acting towards you. I've been unfair and snarky and bitchy and you've...you've been so patient with me." He's blubbering now, his large body shaking with emotion. My heart goes out to him and I, too, am crying.

I stroke his pale hair and say, "Because I knew that it wasn't really you saying all those negative things. That you were hurting after John died and then Mom, and all that guilt you felt inside. You were taking it out on me because I was the closest person for you to lash out at."

"How come..." he asks between sobs, "you're so wise?"

"Because I felt angry, too. I felt guilty, crazy guilt about the tough love thing we were doling out to John. Those goddam meetings we were going to that encouraged us to look out for ourselves more and not pander to him and stop the co-dependency...you know, I felt mad at myself because I didn't call him back that time - like if I'd been there more for him he wouldn't have taken that overdose. I was mad at you because you and he had had that fight... and worst of all? I felt mad at Mom for abandoning us - even though it wasn't her fault. Can you imagine? I felt furious at her for *dying* – how screwed-up is that?"

Anthony wheezes out a little laugh. "I guess we're both as fucked-up as each other, huh? We probably need several sessions with a therapist. Can we be friends now? Can you forgive me for being such a jackass?"

I squeeze him tightly and say, "Of course I forgive you and we have always been friends, no matter what. I have never given up on you, Ant. Ever."

We nestle in each other's warm embrace. I feel the softness of his pink silk pajamas and smile. What a pair we are. He - the consummate drama queen and I, a basket-case disaster in every possible way. I can't hold a deal together, have hand-picked a stalking Frenchman as my future husband who probably murdered his father, and I don't even know if I'm bisexual or if I can even ever have sex with a man and his penis again.

Anthony's breath hitches from his weeping, he draws back from me asking suddenly, "Well, did you call her back last night and ask for details - about her accusations about Sophie? Proof?"

"Call who back?"

"Laura, of course."

Oh okay, so we are back to that conversation. Heartfelt sibling reunion over. Fine.

"I didn't have time," I answer. "The second after I'd listened to Laura's message, Alexandre and I had that crazy car chase and then he threw me over his shoulder and took me to Van Nuys Airport to catch the private jet to Vegas. I didn't have a second."

"And then you escaped through the toilet window."

"Exactly."

"Leaving your cell behind with her number on it so you can't call her back."

"Yes."

"Laura could be making it up or accusing Sophie of something she never did."

"Whose side are you on, Anthony? You sound like Alexandre! I'm going to end up in an asylum like in one of those psychological horror movies where nobody believes the heroine and sends her stark-raving mad!"

"Sorry, just I haven't met this Sophie but I have to admit she does have a pretty face from photos and looks kind of nice."

I pound a feather cushion with my fists to stop myself from smashing my brother in the face. "Shut up!" I yell.

"Sorry but all this is kind of… I mean, Alexandre loves you, right? He must *know* his own sister. If she were really going to harm you physically, he'd stop her in her tracks."

"She stabbed her own father in the groin, Anthony."

"After he'd repeatedly raped her and beaten her – the father had it coming to him."

"That's exactly what Alexandre always says."

"What happened to their dad anyway? Where is he now?"

"Oh, right, get this…he just 'disappeared'."

Anthony laughs. "Wow, you really are entangled in a family affair, aren't you? You think Sophie killed their father?"

"Maybe," I reply, secretly thinking that Alexandre was in on it too, but not daring to say that to Anthony. I think of how Alexandre mixed rat poison with his father's food when he was only a small child. Killing him could have been the next step. Alexandre could be capable of anything, especially recently with all his money and power. He could have even paid someone to do it for them. And that's why Sophie has such a hold on him. They share a guilty secret. I'm wondering at what point the father disappeared. Hmm…it would be interesting to know that.

Anthony breaks my train of thought, "It sounds to me as if, deep down inside, you *like* the fact that your fiancé could be a killer."

I stare at him incredulously. "What?" *Can Anthony read my mind? How does he know I think Alexandre could be guilty of murder?*

My brother raises his pale blond eyebrows. "Who are your favorite movie characters?"

I roll my eyes. "What's that got to do with any of this?"

"You love fucked-up tough guys, Pearl, let's face it. You like bad boys, menacing, unscrupulous men."

"Alexandre is not bad, he's sweet and kind."

"Who are your favorite movie characters?" he sing-songs. "Travis Bickle and Michael Corleone, aren't they? I think that says it all, don't you?"

"Okay, I love Robert de Niro and Al Pacino just because they are great actors, nothing more."

"No, what you love most is the mysteriously sinister characters they portray, their ice-cold, ruthless interiors mixed with their dark, brooding, panty-melting eyes. The irresistible villain. Well, in *The Godfather* and *Taxi Driver* Bobby and Al were in their prime, of course – they're grandfathers now but–"

"Alexandre's eyes are green, anyway," I interrupt.

Anthony takes a swig of coffee. "Your fiancé doesn't have me fooled for a second. Oh, he's Mr. Perfect on the *exterior*, alright, with his textbook French manners, opening doors for ladies and pulling out your chair at dinner and giving to charity et cetera et cetera, but *within* him lurks a dangerous man, believe me. Let's face it, you've always gone for the typical bad boy."

"That is so not true! Brad wasn't a bad boy."

"He started fooling around on you and you gave him the perfect out by having that little adventure with those footballers. Which means, maybe he wasn't bad *enough* for you. You sabotaged the relationship because you secretly found him boring."

"How d'you know about the footballers, *anyway*, I never told you."

"I overheard Mom talking on the phone to you."

"You *eavesdropped?*"

"You know how she used to whisper so loudly that it attracted attention? That, '*no you don't say*' voice she had that made you instantly stop what you were doing and prick up your ears? Well, she had that voice on when she was on the phone to you, and I....well, I just overheard, that's all. You were not cut out to be the perfect doctor's wife anyway, Pearl."

A wave of sadness engulfs me remembering my mother and I feel heaviness weigh down my heart like a dull ache. "Well Saul was good. He wasn't a bad boy."

"Oh no? Mr. Tax Evasion himself! They nearly sent him to jail and would have if you hadn't bailed him out. But again, he wasn't bad *enough* for you so you divorced him, and that's why you're so crazy about Alexandre and so addicted to him. He's your Michael Corleone."

I think back to my conversation with my mom and how she was always there for my problems; I could tell her anything, she was like a sister to me. I'm tempted to share my saga of the recurring nightmares with Anthony and reveal the real story of what happened with the rapist footballers, but I keep my mouth closed. The thought of my brother knowing anything about my sexual life repels me. "Listen," I yawn, "I need to get some sleep; I can hardly keep my eyes open."

"Your bed is all made up with fresh sheets. The bathroom has everything you need. I'll guard the front door as I'm sure Mr.

Possessive will be knocking at it any moment now. But don't worry, he'll need a warrant first, I won't let him in."

"I don't know what to do next, Anthony. I'm being cruel to him – he'll be worried about me."

"Let him suffer for a while. He needs to understand you mean business about getting that nut-job sister out of your life first. If you don't stand your ground now, the next thing you know she'll be moving in to your apartment."

I flinch. Needless to say I haven't shared the worst of it with Anthony about my adventure with Alessandra. The too-close-for-comfort mess I got myself into, never mind the kinky business. Curiosity killed the cat, that's for sure.

"Just get some sleep and then we'll think of the next step," my brother continues, his voice sounding sensible. "Meanwhile, I need to call the office. This is the second time in two weeks I've played hooky."

I take a long, hot shower, then collapse into bed and fall into a profound sleep, not dreaming about needle-dick or any nightmares at all but hot, hot sex with Alexandre. I hear myself coming in my sleep, feel the damp heat between my legs - wanting him, yearning for him. He's fucking me from behind, me on top, me underneath, Cowboy style, 69 – every which way and I can't get enough. His soft dark hair is flopping about his face which is beaded lightly with sweat. I can smell him, even his cock I have in my mind's eye, hard as a rock, fucking me, making me come in thunderous spasms. I'm hungry for him, ravenous for his touch, for him to be inside me. I'm moaning in my sleep. I need him. Want. Desire. A burning passion has me on fire.

Can I be strong? Keep my resolve? Or am I so addicted to him that I'm a lost cause?

13

Several hours later, while Anthony is working from home, I slip out the back door and use the neighbor's entrance in their garden to make my exit. I still don't know what to do about Alexandre. I need more time to think before I call him. I'm in love with him, no doubt about it and I want to marry him but every time I'm tempted to give in I think of my naked body sprawled in a ditch, or in a shallow grave. Dead. Maybe even chopped up and distributed all over the United States. Or perhaps Sophie would meddle with the brakes of my car or slip cyanide in my drink. She has people working on her payroll all over the country – she could do anything.

I spend a couple of hours at Anthony's gym, swimming – letting out all my steam and stretching my aching limbs from that long car journey last night. The water feels great and I feel so much better afterwards.

As I'm approaching Anthony's neighbor's back yard, carefully looking out for Alexandre, I hear steady footsteps behind me. My heart is racing, I feel a spike of adrenaline rush through my veins and turn around. It's HIM. He's standing there in jeans and a white T-shirt looking beyond stunning. His jaw is set firm and he has a five o'clock shadow and hooded eyes of a man who hasn't slept all night. He's not smiling. His face is stern, unflinching but he doesn't look angry, just immovable. Uh oh, this is scarier than anything.

I walk over to him, stretch out my arms to hug him, donning a limp smile. But he steps back as if he doesn't want me to touch him. His body language shocks me.

"Alexandre, I'm so sorry, I didn't know what to do last night."

"Oh, I think you did, Pearl. You had it all nicely planned out. You knew exactly what you were doing."

I edge closer but he steps aside, narrowing his eyes at me. All I can think of is how handsome he is and that I don't want to lose him. "I'm sorry, I—"

"Did you stop for even one second to think how I'd feel? Can you imagine what an idiot I looked; standing there with a lady's handbag while my fiancée had climbed through the window of a fucking *toilet?* To escape from me? How debasing that was?"

"I had no choice, I—"

"I wanted to *marry* you, Pearl. I wanted for us to be together forever - didn't that mean anything to you?"

Oh my God! He's speaking in the past tense!

"Alexandre, I still want to marry you, I still want to make this work, I still—"

"Pearl, don't you get it? It's too late for that now. I can't be with a woman who's going to bolt on me every time my sister does something that she isn't a thousand percent okay with. What kind of a man do you think I am? That I'd abandon my own family for some crazy notion of yours that my sister's got it in for you, that she's going to kill you? It's just insane."

"She is!" I yell. "Laura called me. She told me not to go to Vegas, that Sophie caused her accident—"

"The night the accident happened, when Laura tripped down the stairs, Laura was tipsy and yes, it was Sophie who had taken us both out to dinner and ordered that extra bottle of wine... so was Sophie responsible? No she wasn't, but at the time Laura felt angry – she has two left feet and was always tripping up and usually never drank alcohol, but Sophie didn't ply her with wine on *purpose* so she'd have an accident – you must have misinterpreted what Laura said."

"I didn't! Laura said on the phone last night that—"

"Well we'll never know exactly what Laura said," he interrupts, "because your phone's missing. I was in such a state last night, calling the police - who didn't fucking want to know, by the way - so I had to hire private detectives to try and find you. I was out of my mind with worry. I thought something could have happened. Anyway, I'm sorry, but with all the commotion I left your handbag by a take-out place in LA near the police station, and when I went back for it, it was gone. Stolen. Don't worry, I've already reported it all missing—"

"Alexandre—"

"And I know your phone was inside because straight after the toilet escape fiasco I tried to call you and you can imagine the surprise when it rang in your fucking handbag. I had a look to see what else was there. Your wallet, everything left behind. I figured, a woman who leaves her fiancé without her credit cards and cell phone is a woman who's on the run. As if I were some wife-beating bastard who wanted to hurt you - someone you had to run and hide from."

"No! It wasn't like that. But I was scared. Scared to go near Vegas. I'm still scared of Sophie. Laura was serious. Your sister wants me out of your life, she—"

"Sophie would never hurt you, chérie, believe me."

"I wanted you to stop her to—"

"Imagine yourself in my shoes, Pearl. You and your only brother. You'd abandon Anthony just like that? He's behaved like an asshole with you ever since I met him, yet you have still stood by him because he is your *flesh and blood.* You can't just trash your own family! My sister and I have been through Hell and back together and we're close. But that doesn't seem to register with you. Yet I still listened to you. I have made so many concessions. I have even started to dissolve my own fucking company for you. Even agreed to sell HookedUp to Sophie so I will be out of it one hundred percent. But you know what, Pearl? I'm done. What you did to me last night pushed me to my limit. You demonstrated to me, loud and clear, that you *do not want me* and you know what else? I think you're using Sophie as an excuse. An excuse to run from me."

My heart is pounding. I can't believe what I'm hearing. He is dumping me! Dumping me in favor of his crazy sister.

"I love you Alexandre. Please. Please let's work this out."

"Work what out? As long as Sophie is breathing you're going to nag on and on at me about her. What do you want me to do? Have her killed? So you can be free of her?"

"No, of course not. I just wanted her out of your business."

"And then what? The next step will be you demanding that I don't see her at all. What has she actually *done* to you? Called you a cougar. Ooh, how terrible! It's her manner, Pearl, she has a sharp tongue. If you only knew some of the stuff she's said to me over the years you'd laugh out loud—"

"She called me a stalker and said you didn't give a shit about me, that I was frigid and...and..."

"But that was over four months ago - she apologized several times and has been trying to make up for it ever since – she's been trying, Pearl. Somebody who buys their future sister-in-law a one-of-a-kind Zang Toi wedding dress is not going to try and hurt you."

"She's been messing with my mind, sneaking in on my movie deal—"

"She came in on a bad movie deal that was sinking to save our asses! Why did she bail out Samuel Myers? Not just because she saw a good business opportunity but because *you and I fucked up.* We hadn't done our homework. Samuel Myers was going broke! Yes, that's right, the whole movie would have gone under because Samuel Myers wasn't good for the money so Sophie came in to make things right. He told you, himself, that he was having financial difficulties but you wouldn't have it, wouldn't believe him. You were so obsessed with Sophie doing a number on you that you wouldn't listen to reason."

"At what point did Sophie get involved?" I'm still trying to work out the Alessandra connection.

"I don't know exactly but the timing was perfect for us all. Why did Sophie not tell us both, earlier? To save us from embarrassment. She thought she could subtly stay in the background and not get involved, except financially. She knew how much this project meant to you. And why did Samuel Myers, himself, not mention it earlier? Because of his pride. He's a big shot producer, or at least was 'till some deal went sour – he was hardly going to admit to you his state of affairs."

My brain is racing a thousand miles an hour. "But that doesn't make sense. It was my idea to have a woman for the role, my idea to take a chance on a gay actress."

"Exactly, Sophie knew all that, knew how you wanted a woman, a more mature actress to play the lead – you'd mentioned that to her yourself at some point – why do you think Samuel Myers was so open to the idea? Because he didn't have a choice. But as far as a gay actress was concerned it was Samuel Myers who put the idea of Alessandra Demarr into your head, wasn't it? When Sophie found out about the mess he was in she took the opportunity to use Alessandra as leverage to make it all work out for everybody. And yes, now I realize that my sister did have an ulterior motive – to give Alessandra a chance to break into the movies – Sophie was giving her a leg up with her career. Sophie was doing all of us a fucking favor by coming on board. Me, you, Sam Myers, Alessandra – all of us would benefit."

"Why did Alessandra pretend she didn't know Sophie?" I ask with suspicion.

"Because Sophie hasn't come out of the closet. She doesn't want her marriage breaking up. She doesn't want her step-daughter knowing she's gay - Elodie has no idea. Alessandra was being discreet."

"Did *you* know about Alessandra, that she and Sophie were lovers?"

"No, of course not or I would have said something when I saw how flirtatious she was being with you. Sophie never discusses her sex life with me anyway, why would I have known about Alessandra?"

I stammer, "She….Sophie…she had it all worked out…to demean me. To get her girlfriend to seduce me so I looked like a fool."

"You're really scraping the barrel now, aren't you, Pearl. She got Alessandra on board the movie because a.) she was cheap and b.) she wanted her girlfriend to get a leading role in a film. Alessandra was basically going to do the part for free as long as she could rework the script. That was the deal. The fact that you then got into Alessandra's panties had nothing to do with Sophie."

"I didn't get into her panties, she got into mine!"

"Six of one, half a dozen of the other, what difference does it make – you two made out, which, by the way, Sophie has no idea about."

"Bullshit! Sophie set me up! They were in on it together."

"Oh please. You think my sister is into BDSM after what she went through with our father? Or she'd want her own girlfriend fooling about with another woman? With whips and shit?"

"To punish me to–"

"Oh come on, Pearl, you've been gagging for a spanking ever since I've known you. You were up for it, Alessandra didn't force you."

I'm lost for words but know that I must be right somehow. I'm all tongue-tied but blurt out, "Sophie was mean to me when she and Elodie came for dinner, she was hinting that things were going to go wrong to 'unravel' themselves and…"

"You know Sophie's English is bad and the translation comes out all wrong sometimes."

I'm standing there stupefied. Everything Alexandre is saying makes sense yet…

"Come here, chérie. Let me give you one last kiss before we say goodbye."

What?? Goodbye? I can feel my breath short, my stomach churning with terror. He's leaving me. This is real. Anthony was right, I should have snapped Alexandre up when I had the chance. *Oh my God!*

He walks towards me and holds me tightly in his arms and then runs his fingers through my swimming pool-wet hair and says, "I'll miss you baby, but there's no way you and I are going to work out. I don't want to play this cat and mouse game any longer. I want a stable relationship, I'm not into roller-coaster rides, sorry."

"You're splitting up with me?"

"*You* split us up last night, Pearl. Not me. You. You broke my heart. You made it clear that our two orange halves will have to go their own separate ways."

"No! That's not what I want at all!"

"You can say what you like, baby, but actions speak louder than words. You made your choice when you escaped out of that toilet window last night, leaving a waiting jet and a waiting fiancé like two pieces of discarded trash. Not to mention the reverend in Vegas, and a special surprise I had planned after our wedding."

"What surprise?"

"It doesn't matter now, it's water under the bridge, it's the past."

The past? No, this can't be happening!

He tilts my head back and kisses me. He presses his lips firmly on my mouth and I open it, craving his tongue, desperate for him, his taste, his everything. I wrap my arms around his back and hold him as close as is feasibly possible. Tears are burning in my eyes; my heart feels as if it's ablaze. Our kiss gets deeper, more ravenous. Tingles dance in my groin, my panties are slick – I need him. I need him inside me, our bodies to be one – I need for us to make love. "Please, Alexandre, give me another chance," I breathe into his mouth.

He pulls me off him slowly but with a firm grip. "No."

"Is that all you can say? No?"

He steps backwards but stops and says, "Bye, Pearl. Keep that Mercedes, by the way. I bought it for you - bought it from the rental company, I figured you needed a car. They'll be in touch. Later today you'll receive a package from me. A new handbag, cell phone and other stuff. The diamond ring is yours to keep. And I've bought you a covered parking space around the corner from your apartment in Manhattan so you won't have to move the Mercedes all the time when they do street cleaning – you know, otherwise you'll end up with millions of parking tickets. Oh yes, I got you a pretty condo near Cap d'Antibes overlooking the Mediterranean – not far from where we stayed at the Hotel du Cap-Eden-Roc; the deeds are in your name. In case you fancy a vacation now and then. You'll love it. It comes with a parking spot, too, because the royal blue Porsche that you drove that lives in my house in Provence? She's yours now – drive her with care. I'll have her delivered there."

I can't believe what I'm hearing. Is this all a joke?

But he continues on in a monotone, hardly stopping for breath. "Oh, and of course your Jim Dine and everything you've left at my apartment, your clothes and books and stuff I'm having delivered to your new place on the Upper East Side. I'm renting somewhere for you because of your apartment being sublet. If you prefer it, let me know and I'll buy it for you. Oh yes, and HookedUp Enterprises? I've done a sweet deal with Natalie. Sweet for her, that is, not me. You and she will be partners, fifty/fifty – I thought you'd be more comfortable that way. I know how you feel about Hollywood and the movie business so you can get back to doing what you're truly good at – documentaries. My lawyers will send all the paperwork to you. You decide if the business idea appeals or not."

I'm speechless, my jaw drops, my eyes are stinging with tears about to flood out at any moment. He has had this all *planned out*. Spent the day organizing everything to buy me off! He's breaking up with me and giving me a 'divorce' settlement all in one go. There's no going back now, he's serious. I start sobbing. I think about Rex – no more walks in the park with him. My life as I know it is over - *I've lost Alexandre forever.*

A voice from above shouts into the garden, "What the fuck is going on down there? What have you done to my sister?" It's Anthony leaning out of his living room window glowering at Alexandre. But Alexandre ignores him.

"Bye Pearl, take care." Alexandre squeezes my hand and walks off with purpose as if he can't get away from me fast enough. The fact that he has been so generous when he didn't have to be has made it all so much worse. I collapse on the lawn and roll into a fetal position howling with painful tears as if someone has stabbed me in the heart.

Because someone just has.

14

The only good thing that has come of this black hole in my life is my rekindled relationship with Anthony. We are closer than we ever have been - even before our mother died. He has made a three hundred and sixty degree turnaround – we have talked things through; the anger, the guilt, the blame on both sides about John. I'm clinging to him like never before.

Right now he's my lifeline.

I stayed on several more days with him in San Francisco, moping about his apartment mainly, nursing my wounds. Alexandre only called once, to check a delivery had arrived: a beautiful red, Hermès Birkin handbag, replete with gift vouchers for Neiman Marcus and Barneys ('to replace make-up or anything lost – about time you had a bag that suited you', his note said) a new Smartphone and the keys to my new apartment. After making sure the number was going through okay, he hung up. He was polite but matter-of-fact as if I meant nothing to him at all.

I wailed for hours, cradling my designer bag like a dog with a bone – a sad reminder of what a fool I'd been to crawl through that ladies' room window. Surely I could have done things differently? No wonder he'd had enough. Normal people don't escape through toilet windows. Normal people don't behave the way I have done.

A Birkin – all those times I'd been going about with my over-sized handbag and now, finally, this one was perfect. Still big enough to fit everything I needed inside but so stylish and chic. The perfect pocketbook named after the Francophile British actress, Jane Birkin, who fell in love with the sexy French singer, Serge Gainsbourg. It brought back with nostalgia the moment when *Je T'aime….Moi Non Plus* was playing, after Alexandre had dressed up as a fireman and just before he asked me to marry him.

He sent me the perfect purse at a price, not because of how expensive those bags are but the price of unhappiness - a continual *aide memoire* of the fool that is me, Pearl Robinson. Ms. Pearl Robinson. I held the Birkin close to me and started crying again. How I wished I could turn back time. He wanted to make me Pearl Chevalier and all I could do was run.

I knew then that I could not possibly accept any of these 'pay-off' gifts – I called to say I wanted to give everything back but he never picked up.

Just when I was thinking that the world couldn't get worse,

Hurricane Sandy struck. Entire coastal stretches along the east side of the country were destroyed, five million without power, and the death toll rising daily. Scores of people died in New York City alone, more than in any other previous natural disaster to have occurred there.

It quickly shook me out of my self-pity, realizing that I was/am one of the lucky ones in the world. Natalie, not so. Her aunt was a victim of the superstorm's wrath. She lived in Queens in a neighborhood which was first ravaged by flood waters before a raging fire burned everything to the ground leaving nothing but a pile of ashes, debris of wrecked cars and dead trees reflected in the oily, knee-deep water.

Natalie is broken-hearted. I thought of what Alexandre had said a couple of weeks earlier when we were talking about choices we make in life and he said something like: *"Maybe Natalie's had a relatively lucky life. Perhaps she's never been a victim of circumstance or ever had to battle with personal demons."*

Poor Natalie, she's certainly been a victim of circumstance now and will be haunted by demons for the rest of her life.

When Bruce arrived back from visiting his parents, I knew it was time to leave. I had options. Go back to New York and settle into my new apartment, the one Alexandre has organized for me. Luckily, the Upper East Side is still in working order, not the case for some other parts of Manhattan where the storm wreaked havoc. I had only seen photos of the apartment, a stunning two bedroom pre-war co-op just around the corner from where my place is (which is sublet for another ten months and I can't break the contract). He said he'd buy it for me if I liked it. I can't even imagine what it would cost, but a lot, and I don't feel comfortable with all these 'gifts' he has showered me with – I want to return them: a condo in the South of France, two incredible cars, a parking space in the city. Things which remind me of him, remind me that I played it all wrong – that I screwed up yet again. Things which I don't deserve.

Another option for me was to drive across America. I had to take the Mercedes to New York so I thought I might as well make a trip out of it.

At one point Daisy said that she and Amy would come too, because Johnny was on business in Phoenix, but then it was cancelled so she changed her mind. A ten day drive just with me on my own didn't appeal at all, especially with the way I'm feeling right now.

I spoke to Natalie several times and she advised me to stay away from New York, just for now. Meanwhile, all she wants to do is spend time with her family.

The third option was to visit my father in Kauai, which is what I decided to do.

That's right, Alexandre *did* call a second time but only briefly to ask what arrangements I had for the Mercedes and how I was planning to take it back to New York. I told him I didn't want the car but he was adamant I keep it. He came up with a plan. Elodie and a friend of hers were going to fly to San Francisco, pick it up, and deliver it to New York for me. They'd drive across the country, very carefully, he'd instructed them, with utmost respect for the car, he'd warned. I consider it his car, anyway; his money paid for it. Elodie and her friend stayed with Anthony and Bruce for a couple of nights before setting off on a sightseeing trip of a lifetime. By that point I had left for Kauai.

So here I am now at my father's in his romantic house made of bamboo, away from the aftermath of Hurricane Sandy, away from the aftermath of my messed-up life. 'At least you're still *alive*,' Anthony reminded me. 'And not, as you feared,' he said, 'some victim of Sophie's.' Perhaps he had a point.

I have thought about Sophie a lot. Mulled over everything. Maybe Alexandre is right...I'm paranoid, being unfair, I've watched too much *Dexter* and *CSI* on TV. Whatever, I made my bed and have to lie in it now. He doesn't want me back. I could hear it in his voice when we spoke those two times. Businesslike - polite but cold. Unemotional. How it kills me to hear him talk to me that way.

Now I spend the days looking at the ocean, watching the waves rise and fall, listening to the surf and sound of birds. I have penned several letters to Alexandre. Not emails but real letters on paper. But they end up in the trash, crumpled up – like my thoughts, confused, shocked, as if the last five months have been one long dream, as if this phantom Frenchman never existed at all, that he was just a figment of my imagination.

Speaking of dreams, I am possessed. Not by needle-dick and company. No. That seems to be over. I am possessed, obsessed by Alexandre. Not only does he occupy my thoughts in the waking hours, but when I close my eyes, too. Constantly there. He is in my subconscious, my conscious, flowing through my veins, beating in my heart. He is everywhere. I see his peridot-green eyes sparkling with happiness looking down on me while I sleep. But when I open my lids, there is emptiness; my soul is like a void of black, a deep, dark cavern of misery. Misery I brought upon myself.

I have been trying to reach Laura all this time. I even asked Elodie if she could get her number for me, I was that desperate. Finally, I got it and left Laura a message but she hasn't called back. I need answers. Is Alexandre just in denial? Denial about how crazy Sophie is, or was he speaking the truth? Whatever, I realize that I was no match for his beloved sister. As Anthony pointed out, I am the water and she is the blood. Ironic that. *Blood is thicker than water* doesn't exist in French yet Alexandre is taking every word of that to heart, polishing each letter of that phrase like a soldier polishing his boots. Until it gleams and shines like a mirror. *Blood is thicker than water.*

"What's up, Pearl?" I nearly jump out of my skin but it's only my dad coming up behind me. He lays his warm hands on my shoulders and gives me a little squeeze. "You've been very silent lately, sweetie, very introvert – that's not like you at all."

I turn around, holding one of his hands on my now bony shoulder – I can hardly eat at the moment. "I'm sorry Dad, sorry I'm being so dull and boring."

I look up at his handsome, rugged face. His sand-blond hair falls limp about his high cheekbones, his crow's feet are etched in hard lines about his dark blue eyes which reveal a man who has lived life. Suffered and pushed himself to the limits. His face is a map. He has a reckless air about him mixed with a soft vulnerability which makes him hard to resist. I think about Natalie and see how she must have fallen head over heels in love with him but ran because she needed to protect herself. He could break a heart because you want more from him and he isn't able to give more. He is a self-absorbed person, yet kind and caring. Self-absorbed because it's hard to penetrate his shell. *What is he thinking?* she must have wondered, *why can't he open up?*

"It's time you learned how to surf," he says in his deep voice.

God he's handsome. I suppose I'm not meant to notice things like that because he's my father - but I'm not blind. Natalie must be crazy about him however much she's in denial.

"What happened between you and Natalie?" I ask, ignoring the surf request. He has been pushing that one on me for as long as I can remember.

"I tried, sweetie, I tried."

"Why did she come running back to New York so soon, then? What did you do?"

He lets out a sigh. "The way I see it? She was scared. Scared by her strong feelings for me. Natalie is a woman who has always been in control of situations. She's a tough business woman, a negotiator. She wanted to negotiate me, didn't want to lose herself in me."

"So you were hard on her?"

"Not at all. I felt that she was trying to manipulate me into being somebody I wasn't."

"She's so beautiful," I say.

"She's that, alright."

I frown. "Poor thing. Hurricane Sandy has really knocked the wind out of her. I was going to go back to New York to help her in any way I could but she wants just to be with her family."

My dad answers sadly, "I've called her several times to try and comfort her but I guess she's just not willing to talk about it. She still won't return my calls."

I sit there pensively, his hands still cupping my shoulders. The view is spectacular – a carpet of emerald green stretching to the deep blue of the ocean ahead. Coconut palms sway like ballet dancers in the gentle breeze and a cockerel crows for the fourth time in a row. An early morning mist is rising almost like smoke it's so thick, dissipating into the air as it ascends into the cobalt blue of ice-clear sky. It's just after dawn. As usual, I couldn't sleep and my father has gotten up early so he can get in some surf time.

"Come with me, honey. Come and surf. Surfing will clear your mind – it's the zen of life. Surf and all your troubles will melt away."

"It's your addiction, isn't it?"

"It's my sanity, Pearl."

"Maybe tomorrow."

And then he does something that he has never done before with me. His voice deepens into a commanding, strict tone. He suddenly sounds like an old-fashioned father from the Victorian age who might spank his children or put them to bed with no supper. "No, Pearl. I've had enough of you moping around like some lovesick, surly teenager. You are *coming surfing* and that's the bottom line." He clutches my hand and pulls me up out of my chair with a strong jerk.

I stand there stupefied.

He barks, "You are my *daughter* and I'm going to make you a surfer, once and for all. When you next see that French boyfriend of yours you can show him just how good you are. Give him something to be impressed about. You think he'd like to see you as you've been all week, hunched over in that chair staring at waves all day long? Or making work calls? No, honey, he was attracted to an active girl full of *joie de vivre* when he met you - a woman who went rock-climbing on that first date. Show him what you're made of."

"It's no good, Dad. It's over between us. He doesn't want me now. He's not going to give me another chance."

"Nonsense. You're coming surfing, young lady. Soon you won't even be brooding about him anymore anyway - you'll have better things to occupy your mind."

I pull back but he keeps yanking me toward him. "Besides, have you seen the talent out there?" he continues. "Have you set eyes on the bodies along that beach?"

"What do you mean?" I ask, still surprised by his sudden air of authority.

"There are, like, at least ten dudes on that beach who are good enough to compete around the world. You think your French guy is handsome and can surf? Wait until you set your eyes on this bunch of kids."

"Kids?"

"There are some good-looking young men out there, some in their late twenties, early thirties – perfect for you if you're attracted to younger guys - a few of them interesting, too. Everybody thinks surfers are dumb but we're not, we have the key to the secret treasure box, the potion to the essence of life."

I've heard all this before but I listen anyway. I watch him as he continues with his spiel.

"Meanwhile, most other people out there are too busy running about in a rat-race in some concrete jungle somewhere, so preoccupied with 'ambition' and getting ahead that they can't appreciate what real living is all about. We surfers know - we have the wisdom." He tells me this with an ironic smile, although what he says he truly believes from the bottom of his heart.

"Surfers with brains?" I tease, although my dad is extremely smart. He can tell you anything about philosophy or astronomy and is an ace at mathematics. You wouldn't know it, though. At first sight he's so startlingly 'cool' and so buffed-up you'd take him for…for what? An old hippie? No, he's too in shape for that, his eyes too focused. An ex-bodyguard? No, he's too graceful, too ethereal. Who is he? I wonder to myself. I observe the flexing of his biceps as he turns his surfboard upside down. His fifty-nine year-old body could pass for thirty-five. A thirty-five year-old in great shape, no less.

I reflect on what Alexandre said about living in a tree-house and wonder, is that what my dad is doing, basically? Not that his bamboo house is a shack, no – it's pretty state-of-the-art and modern; he designed and built it himself. But living the simple life, no frills, no 'needs'. He doesn't care about the car he drives or impressing anyone. He is who he is and he makes no excuses for himself.

He squints his eyes as he gazes at my left hand. My engagement ring is making reflections on the walls and ceilings like a mirror, twinkling in the morning light. "But take that rock off your finger, first," he tells me, "or it could get washed away with the pull of the surf. I have a safety deposit box in the house - you can put it in there." I am still wearing the ring even though it's officially over between Alexandre and me, as if the ring is a symbol of hope that somehow everything will work itself out. He refused to take it back. So I carry it about on my finger like a wish.

My dad and I leave the porch to its spectacular view and go inside. My father taking me in hand the way he has is almost a relief. I don't have to think anymore; he can do my thinking for me. Isn't that what parents are for sometimes? To ease the pain? To shake you out of a stupor?

"Change into a whole piece swimsuit or you could scratch your belly on the board," he advises me, waxing up his surfboard.

"All I have is that bright red Baywatch-type thing from years ago."

"So? What's wrong with that?"

I raise my eyebrows. "I'll look like a Pamela Anderson wannabe. I'll attract attention."

"You'll attract attention no matter what, honey. They all want to meet you."

"*What?*"

"You think it's normal that you live by the ocean and you've been tucked up in hiding in this house for nearly ten days? Every morning when I go down the boys are asking where you are. They're curious. Curious to meet my only daughter. Besides, I need your help at the shop today. We'll surf all morning, have lunch and then you can help me organize my book keeping. Your lady of leisure days are over, Pearl. From now on, it's hang out in my shop, surf, or swim. No more moping about. Is that a deal?"

"Okay, it's a deal," I agree and then my mouth breaks into a huge grin.

"That's better. That's what I want to see. I want to see that big, beautiful smile of yours."

15

The surfer guys are really friendly and greet me with a warm welcome as if the top of the hill where my father lives were on a different planet. Their dedication to the surf is as forceful as the Pacific waves, unrelenting - they don't venture far from the beach during the day.

My surf lesson begins on the sand, itself, and then once in the ocean I find out that 'paddle' is the magic word. With my torso pressed on the board, I paddle with my arms feverishly out to sea and am then spun around by my father at the right moment to catch the wave and ride it to the shore. The idea is to stand up on the board as soon as possible. Easy on land, but nigh impossible with a fast-moving crashing wave. I do several tries, toppling over immediately into the water, each try more exhausting than the last, especially after the paddling; my arms and shoulders feel as if they are about to snap off, but in the end, after a long morning, I get there and I manage to ride the wave upright on my shaky legs all the way to the beach.

"Not bad for your first try," my father says approvingly. "Not bad at all."

"I don't know if I'm cut out for this, Dad," I say looking off to the rolling green hills in the distance and then back at him. "It's really hard, all that paddling – I'm wiped out. No wonder you surfers have such big pecs and biceps."

"It's just a question of building up your stamina, honey, that's all. What d'you make of the kids here? Anyone that takes your fancy?" he asks, gesticulating at the guys expertly riding the waves.

"Where are all the girls? The women surfers?" I reply.

"They're about, just not today. Shame Zac's not here, he's a great teacher. Sometimes it's best when someone who isn't next of kin shows you the ropes," he tells me with a playful grin.

"Who's Zac?"

"You'll see. You won't be able to miss him. He's one of our local champions. He could show you a few tricks of the trade."

Later that evening after dinner, Daisy calls. I can tell immediately by her quivering voice that something is wrong. She usually speaks with such bravado and confidence that I'm instantly troubled.

After both of us have discussed the horror of Hurricane Sandy she blurts out, "Johnny is having an affair."

I take my cell onto the veranda where the reception is clearer. "Wait, hold up, Daisy…an affair or a one-night stand."

"A one-night bloody stand that developed into a full fucking-blown affair!"

Fucking being the operative word, I think. "But that doesn't make sense, Johnny's crazy about you."

Daisy blows her nose into the receiver. "That's what I thought, too, but I was obviously dead wrong. Wrong and blind, to boot. I trusted him."

"Well of course you did. He's your *husband.* You had no reason not to trust him."

"I should have seen the writing on the wall."

"What writing?"

"The increase in the amount of 'business' trips he was making. The stupid cow lives in Phoenix, doesn't she?"

"Phoenix? Who *is* she?" I ask taking in a deep breath.

"Another married woman."

"Oh, my God."

"Which makes it worse. The pair of them are as bad as each other. She has two kids. She has a husband who's just as much in shock as I am."

"You've spoken to the husband?"

"It was him that called me. He was the one who discovered what they were up to."

"How did they meet? What's her name, how old is she? *Why is she doing this?"* I shout out all in one breath.

"The worst? She's not even pretty. I don't understand, Pearl. She's plain, homey-looking, the type that might bake bread. Not that bread bakers can't be attractive, but you know—"

"What's Johnny playing at?" I screech with disbelief.

"You ask me. This has been going on for six months. She's a secretary - oh sorry, not meant to use that word these days…she's a *personal assistant* to one of the guys in Johnny's company. She must give really good blow jobs, or something, because I don't get what he sees in her!"

"You've seen her?"

"Her husband made friends with me on Facebook so I could check out their family photos. Two kids - not to mention Amy. All these little hearts being broken. Can you believe it? The husband is devastated, of course."

"Does Amy know?"

"No, of course not, but even at five years old she's guessed something's up. Mummy can't stop crying, Mummy has got red, swollen eyes, so she knows Mummy is in a terrible way."

"Oh, Daisy, I'm so, so sorry."

"So am I."

"What excuse has Johnny given? I mean, is he in *love* with this woman?"

"He says he needs time."

"So typical - as if you're just meant to sit about twiddling your thumbs while he works out his inner man-whore."

Daisy laughs faintly. "He's still at the apartment. Can't make up his mind what he wants to do."

The *wanting the cake and eating it, too,* syndrome. Sounds familiar. An idea suddenly occurs to me and I say, "Daisy, why don't you and Amy come out here for a break? Get away. The airports are all open again, aren't they?"

"I can't, Daisy's in school and stuff."

"She's only five - it's not the end of the world. What she misses in school she'll make up for by seeing Hawaii. What could be a better education than that? Seeing the Fiftieth State?"

"Tempting, Pearl, but I really can't afford it right now. If I'd known this was coming I'd have saved some 'fuck-you' money."

"It'll be my treat. I'll get your tickets and once you're here it's cheap. We'll eat in – there's not a lot to spend your money on, the surf and sun are free – life's simple here."

"I don't know, I really—"

"Come on," I cajole. "You need a change of scenery. Get away from Johnny. He needs time? You need a vacation!"

"Good point."

"I'm going online as we speak and getting you two tickets."

"Pearl—"

"I won't take no for an answer. Then maybe Johnny will realize what he's missing not having you both at home. It'll give him the kick up the butt he deserves."

"You don't want to listen to me miserably droning on about my problems."

"Oh, please, Daisy, like it isn't always the other way round. As if you haven't had years of me sharing some drama or other of mine while you've sat there patiently giving me wise advice. It's time I did something for you in return."

Finally, after hours of lying awake, staring at the ceiling and wondering how I could have done things differently with Alexandre, I fall asleep. I dream about white surf and 'killer' waves. I'm riding fast on the surfboard moving my body in balance with the swell and Alexandre is watching me from the beach, a proud grin on his handsome face.

So I'm irritated as hell when my happy dream is woken by a

noise. Is it one of those feral pigs? Sometimes they come snuffling and grunting about my father's garden. The legend goes that Captain Cook introduced them to the islands; a source of nourishment for shipwrecked crews. Now they are proving to be a nuisance. The hogs (in their ongoing quest to find something to eat) dig and rootle about in the undergrowth trying to find worms and roots. Whole chunks of land and mountain slopes are being stripped of native vegetation making it easier for invasive weeds like ginger to get established, and the puddles in the mud wallows they create breed mosquitoes with avian malaria that kills the native birds. Hence, their appearance on local restaurant menus.

I lie in bed, stock-still, my ears pricked up like a dog. Scary thoughts of wild, long tusked, razor-backed, boars pillaging my father's garden, breaking and entering the house and attacking me, fill my racing imagination. I decide I should do something and scare them away. I get up and move over to the window and look out. The sky is dark as black ink. I listen. No hog-like sounds at all. No grunting, just a gentle rustling in the bushes.

I nearly have a heart attack when I hear a man's low voice.

It is Alexandre.

"Hi, chérie," he says casually as if no time has passed, as if I had never escaped from the airport ladies' room window.

I lean out of the window into the shadows and catch a glimpse of his face lit up by a waxing moon. My heart is racing so intensely I think my knees are going to give way beneath me.

"What are you doing here?" I ask amazed. "How did you find this place in the dark?"

"I have my ways; modern technology offers all sorts of solutions these days."

"You came," I say simply. "You're not still furious with me

then?"

He bends forward into the open window. His breath is on me, I can taste the smell of him; his Alexandre elixir. "I thought I'd never see you again," I murmur into his face.

"As if," he breathes into my hair. "I could never abandon you, Pearl." His soft mouth presses on mine and he begins to lick along my lips, parting them. But then his gentleness turns like a cat who suddenly becomes over-excited, and he nips my lower lip. I can feel the salty taste of blood.

"I need you, Pearl. I have to make love to you. Don't you know that? I can't live my life without you, without being inside you, without—" He doesn't finish his sentence but continues with his rough kiss, playful and needy all at once. He rams his tongue deep inside my mouth and I groan. I can taste the blood, the sweet saliva of his minty apple breath and I return the kiss with passionate fervor.

"Alexandre," I moan.

"Aren't you going to invite me in?"

"Of course. My father's sleeping so don't make a noise."

"Are you ashamed? Worried he'll disapprove of me?"

"He's not so keen on you right now," I say with a sly grin. "He wants to hook me up with one of the surfers. He doesn't think you deserve me."

"That's why I'm here, baby. I got thinking about what you might do here in Kauai. You think I want my future wife fucking some sexy surfer?"

Tears fill my eyes. *Future wife? So he has forgiven me!* I rush to the front door and open it quietly. He's standing there, legs astride and I fall into his arms. "Alexandre, I've been so miserable without you." *And I think, even if I die from Sophie's hand, I'd rather die than be without him.*

He scoops me in his arms like a baby and carries me inside the house. "Nice place," he whispers approvingly. "I love the huge open-plan space. Great taste your father has."

"He built this house with his own bare hands," I reply proudly. "My room is just around the corner here on the ground floor. Actually, I've just remembered, my dad is out for the night seeing a friend."

"A fuck-buddy type friend? I thought he was dating Natalie."

"She's not interested. Won't return his calls. He's an attractive man, my dad, he can't be expected to live a monk's life."

"No, of course not."

We go into my room and Alexandre lays me gently on the bed, all the while kissing me ravenously. By the time he slips his fingers inside me I am a pool of liquid jelly.

"Always so ready to be fucked by me, aren't you?"

"Yes," I whimper. "I need you even more than you need me."

"The only problem is, Pearl, you've been a really naughty girl."

"I know."

"I'm going to have to punish you."

More feather beating, I think. I know there's no Nutella in the house so...

"This time I mean business, though."

"What kind of business?" I breathe into his hot mouth.

He says seriously, "Look, you know about my fucked-up past. You know how I feel about men hitting women after what that fucker did to my mother and sister—"

"I know, Alexandre, I'm not asking you to—"

"Let me finish," he interrupts. "Secretly I want to raise my hand to you and give you a good hiding." He pauses and then adds, "Let's put it this way, I'm a clandestine Dom, but you must have guessed that about me already with your female intuition."

"I had my suspicions," I admit.

"I want to beat you and then fuck you. Fuck you really hard. I need to punish you for hurting me, Pearl, for humiliating me so badly."

"Why have you kept this Dom side of yourself so secret?" I ask. "It's not as if it's illegal, lots of people—"

"Because I felt ashamed. Ashamed inside. I felt as if I would be betraying my mother in some way, betraying Sophie, too - as if I was psychologically sick ever wanting to hurt a woman in any way."

I can feel a gush of new wetness gather hot and horny between my legs. I want him to do it. I want him to dominate me, to punish me. I want to be all his even if it means getting hurt.

"When you disobey me Pearl, it makes me angry. But it also excites me, gets me hard and makes me want to sort you out, fuck you, punish you and fuck you again." He trails his hand along the nape of my neck and a delicious, shimmering shiver courses along my spine. "Do you understand why I want to punish you?"

"Yes," I whisper.

"You're a spoiled Star-Spangled brat. Independent, testy and always doing what you think best. Not your fault, of course, you American women are born that way. It's in your pioneer blood. But it makes me want to fuck it out of you. Beat that disobedience out of your peachy ass, fuck it out of your tight little pearlette. And I don't want anyone else coming near you," he says with a threatening gaze, eyeing up my Baywatch swimsuit which is slung over a chair. "You've been prancing about in *that?*"

"Yes. All the guys on the beach have been staring at me; it makes my tits look great, you can see my nipples really clearly," I tease knowing that I'm riling his jealous side.

He laughs. "An insecure man would get flustered by that remark, but me? I know it's me you want. All those men can stare at you all they want but it's me you want to fuck. But just to be clear, Pearl. You're mine." He strokes the inside of my thigh with his long fingertips and slips one inside my wet hole. "Do. You. Understand."

He's hovering over me. My high bed is on the same level as his crotch. I take his fly and open it letting his erection spring free and pull his jeans down. No underwear. "Yes, I understand, Alexandre."

"Good girl. Now be an obedient fiancée and suck my cock. Are you over that penis phobia, baby? Do you think you can suck me so I come hot and heavy in your pretty mouth?"

"Oh yes," I murmur. "Oh yes," and I take his erection in my hands and then run my lips over his soft, warm crown. My tongue flickers on his one eyed-jack and I lick off the pre-cum and taste his welcome salty-sweetness. I take his cock and tease my nipples with the top of it and then pop it back into my mouth. My groin is on fire and even more so when he groans and thrusts his hips forward into my face so it goes deeper. "That's right, baby, keep sucking, oh yeah, oh yeah, just like that. I'm going to really fuck you like you've never been fucked before. That little lesbian fiasco? I knew it wouldn't last because you crave cock at the end of the day, don't you, Pearl? You like a huge, hard cock inside you, fucking your hot, tight pearlette, isn't that what you want?"

"Yes, I want 'ock," I say, gagged by his massive size, hardly able to get out the words coherently.

"Whose cock, baby? Whose cock inhabits your brain every waking hour and in every wet dream?" he says rocking his hips forward.

"Yours, Alexandre. Only yours," and I wrap my lips tightly about his huge penis sucking as tight as I can as I claw onto his firm butt with my hands drawing him as close as possible to me.

"Good girl," he groans and I feel him expand inside my mouth. A rush of cum shoots at the back of my throat. He continues to moan and gently thrusts back and forth, fucking my mouth very leisurely as his orgasm slowly fades. I swallow desperately, lapping up every drop, savoring his taste.

"This is just the beginning," he warns. "I haven't finished with you yet."

He pulls out from my mouth and he's still erect. Round two 'coming' up. I run my eyes along his rock-hard abs, that sexy fine line of hair from his belly button seeping into his crotch does things to my brain. He still has a faint tan left over from the summer, his golden skin soft and smooth. I stroke my hands around his ass, his thighs – feel the strength of him, his powerful body, his flexing muscles. I practically come myself just drinking him in (ha, ha, yes I giggle to myself at my pun). Alexandre is Beauty incarnate. I have genuinely never seen a man as handsome as he is. No male model or movie star can compete. He is incredible in every way. It's true; all those pumped-up surfers can stare all they want at me but it's Alexandre I desire.

And only Alexandre.

As I'm gazing at him he suddenly spins me around so I am in

a letter L on the bed, my torso spread out flat and my butt on the edge of the mattress, my feet almost touching the floor. He's standing over me, lording it over my wetness, my trepidation, my excitement. He starts circling my ass softly with his palm and trailing his index finger over my opening, at one point dipping it inside as if it were nectar. I can feel myself clench. Oh wow, I'm so ready for this, whatever 'this' may be. Then he ties my hands together with a silk scarf he seems to have in his jeans' pocket and puts my wrists above my head. Did he plan this? He seems so prepared. He takes my hair and gathers it in his hands, tugging at me so I can't move.

He starts a rhythm, chanting a tune that I learned as a child, a song from the American War of Independence. How does he know this song?

Left, right, left, right left
I left my wife with forty-eight kids
On the verge of starvation without any Johnny cakes
Oops, by golly, by left
Right, left right left....

At the 'left' he smacks me on my left butt cheek and then on my right... wallop! Both with his right hand. His left hand is still fisted in my hair making sure I don't escape. And then, on the last 'left' of the song he crams his erection into me hard and then withdraws immediately. Each time the smarting spanks are a warm-up to what I'm craving more than anything – the hard thrust into my opening on the last 'left'. The pain is bearable…in fact…delectable and I await each plunge.

I'm groaning. Waiting with baited breath, screaming

Alexandre's name. On the next thrust I know I'm going to climax. This is so sensual so...erotic despite the hard stinging slaps. And then it comes, that last hard shove inside me and it tips me into an ecstatic roll of emotional, orgasmic fervor, my brain and Venus ringing and trembling from deep within. This time he doesn't pull out but lets himself rest within me as I spasm around him, my muscles clenching onto his length like a limpet clinging to a rock. He comes too, his enormousness filling my walls, pulsating inside me with his groaning climax as he empties himself with a cry.

"Pearl—"

I hear bells sounding in my ears - no not bells, music so sweet. I blink my eyes. What's the music? It's coming from above. It's *She's a Rainbow* by the Rolling Stones...'she comes in colors everywhere'....

Yes, I think, I come in colors. I see flashes of red and gold - the orgasm is still sparkling within my body lighting me up like a firework display.

I lie there panting and open my eyes from my sexual stupor. It's no longer dark outside but dawn is creeping slowly through the bedroom window. I move my wrists...but wait...why aren't they tied? My eyes fly open and I feel my hands, not above my head but between my hot, wet thighs, my post-orgasm still tingling through my core. My wrists are free. I am not splayed across the bed - no, I am tucked up under the sheets. I turn over to feel for Alexandre. The song is louder now. It's my father's 'alarm' – he likes to wake to music instead of a clock.

I sit up with a jerk. Alexandre is nowhere to be seen.

Of all the nightmares I have had, this is the worst of all.

Because this was nothing but a dream.

16

D aisy and Amy have been here for two days. She is like
the sister I never had and I'm so grateful to have her in
my life. Coming here was just what the doctor ordered.
She needed to get away and gain a little perspective.
Being under the same roof as Johnny, while he procrastinated
about what he wanted or didn't want was not doing her any
favors.

Johnny. Johnny Cakes. Funny how dreams mix up everyday
occurrences and names and places with fantasies. There I was the
other night dreaming about bondage accompanied by an
American Civil War marching song about Johnny Cakes (sung by
a Frenchman, no less). Needless to say, I haven't shared that with
Daisy – a little too bizarre, especially as Johnny played a symbolic
role – *'without any Johnny Cakes.'*

When we walked into my father's house, after I had collected
Daisy and Amy from the airport, I noticed something I hadn't

anticipated:

My father's expression the moment he set eyes on my friend. He has known Daisy for years but hadn't seen her for ages. He wasn't expecting a new, slim version of her. He still had the Annie girl in his mind, the chubby-cheeked redhead. At least, that is what I deduced judging by the way his jaw dropped when she walked through the front door. All he said was, 'My, how fabulous you and Amy both look.' But I could see a sparkle in his eyes. I am not sure how I feel about my friends and co-workers (Daisy and Natalie) being offered up as love fodder for my father. Luckily, Daisy hasn't noticed and I have kept silent. The last thing she needs right now is more complications, but still, nice to have someone be so attentive even if he is twenty years older than she is.

Amy is in Seventh Heaven. Coming from a city it's a big change; she is free to roam about in the garden and when we go down to the beach she has no end of admirers. She has a sassy sense of humor and it isn't long before she has a throng of people gather about her, keen to hear a five year-old's outtake on life. She has an old soul for such a feisty child, and even though she doesn't seem to know what is going on with her parents, she comes out with things like, 'Don't worry, Mom, everything will work out just fine,' and 'Look at the waves, Mom – sometimes nature can be really powerful, more powerful than we are so don't sweat the small stuff.' She has made friends with one of the surfer's children; a little boy named Pete.

As Daisy and I are having a light picnic on the beach and Amy and Pete are busy making sandcastles, Daisy tells me about a new plan she has hatched. Payback for Johnny.

"I'm not actually going to *do* anything, God forbid, but I'm going to let him know how it feels."

"What do you mean?" I ask, trying to catch on to her runaway train of thought. Every day she comes up with something different. A new-fangled plot to punish him.

"I want him to feel what it's like being in my shoes. I'm going to pretend I'm having a fling with a surfer."

I try to suppress a grin. Daisy is being dead serious.

She raises her eyebrows. "Maybe that will shock him into action."

"Yes, but what kind of action? It could make him run into the arms of Mrs. Phoenix all the faster."

"You have a point there."

"The truth is, Daisy, honesty really is the best policy. Playing games is not the best line of action. At least if you are honest with your feelings you can hold your head up high with dignity. Because if you lie to him, or to yourself, it could catch up with you in the end."

"Maybe you're right."

"But at the same time you can't be Johnny's doormat. You need to be strong and have barriers. There are things you have to let him know that are not acceptable. It is not acceptable for him to expect you two to remain under the same roof while he makes up his procrastinating mind."

"I wish I had some of that 'fuck-you' money you told me about. Then I could get my own place."

"Yeah. That's what every woman needs. You never know when things can change. It's always good to be prepared. A woman needs to be like a one-band army. Ready with her ammunition, ready with her armor, yet actively seeking and living a peaceful existence. But if she is attacked emotionally or physically she has the tools – the strength to protect herself."

Daisy pulls her curly red hair into a high ponytail which sets off the cheekbones on her pretty freckled face. "In a perfect world," she says with a sigh.

"I know, easier said than done."

"I'm just not making enough money yet. I have a few clients but I depend on Johnny's income. I can't just get up and leave."

"Such an archetypal scenario," I say. "Women the world over are in this predicament. Worse. Many of them are being physically abused or have five kids to feed. Think about it, Daisy. Maybe you and Amy should move in with me to my new apartment."

"How do you feel about that? Alexandre paying for your apartment when you aren't even with him anymore."

"I told him I couldn't accept it, that I wouldn't move in."

"And what was his response?"

"He said it was too late, that all my stuff had been moved there and if I didn't take it, it would sit there empty. That's why I came here. I needed time to sort my head out. I still don't really know what the next step is."

"Maybe we should all move here to Kauai," Daisy suggests with a giggle. "Life would be so much less complicated."

"That's what my dad keeps telling me."

"So what are you going to do about Alexandre?"

"There's nothing really I *can* do, he's decided for me."

"For your own peace of mind, I think you need to talk with Laura."

"I've tried calling. I've left messages."

"Well maybe you need to go and see her. She might be ignoring your messages because she's scared of Sophie finding out and doesn't want to attract attention to herself. You need to talk to her face to face. Sort out all this Sophie stuff once and for all."

"What difference does it make now? Alexandre and I aren't together anymore."

"You say that, Pearl, but do you remember last time you split up? He came back to you. He was still in love with you. If that happens again, the Sophie problem will still be there. You need to know for sure what happened."

"She tried to kill Laura and pretended it was an accident."

"You really believe Sophie would have *risked* that? That's attempted murder, Pearl. Surely Alexandre would have guessed?"

"Not when it comes to Sophie. He can't see the wood from the trees. He protects her no matter what. His loyalty is unwavering."

"Well, I still think you need to see Laura - one on one."

"Fly to London?"

"You can stay with my mother, she'd be thrilled. I can set you up with some mates of mine – they've all heard about you – all dying to meet my beautiful, American, best friend, Pearl."

"You've told them about me?"

"Yes, of course. Only terrible things, though."

I laugh, then grab a handful of sand and let it run through my fingers like an egg timer. "I need to get back to New York, though. This 'break' has morphed into too long a vacation. But still, at least I've been able to spend time with my family. Anthony and I have patched up our relationship and I've gotten to know my dad better. We've bonded with the surfing. It's been a very healing time for me. Adversity sometimes brings hidden gifts."

"So what's happening with HookedUp Enterprises?" Daisy asks, her eyes fixed on Amy as she rushes towards a wave with her little bucket.

"Natalie and I are carrying on the company. I'll finish *Stone Trooper* which has now started filming."

"Who was the movie star they picked in the end to play the male lead?"

"Nobody famous – the budget simply wasn't available even with Sophie's input. But he's an excellent actor and very handsome. I received the final script. It's good, actually. I think it will turn out well."

"And then what?"

I pour some iced-tea from a thermos flask into a paper cup and hand it to Daisy. "Back to documentaries. There are so many topics that deserve attention."

She takes a sip. "Good for you, Pearl. Do you feel deflated? Disappointed by all this?"

"It's been a learning curve. I always wanted to write scripts but the truth is, there is no better script than real life. Documentaries suit me way more."

"And what about Alexandre? If he came back to you, even if it meant the whole Sophie saga going on forever, would you want him anyway?"

"Some days I feel the answer to that question is a definite 'yes' I'd want him, despite the risks, but I don't know, I think you're right, Daisy. I need to go and see Laura and talk to her face to face. She and Alexandre were together for at least a couple of years. If anyone knows Sophie, she does."

"Well if it isn't Pearl, the jewel of Kauai."

Daisy and I look up abruptly from our girl-talk. A deep voice has interrupted us and for a moment I'm irritated. *Go away, I think. Leave us to our privacy.* But Daisy's mouth hangs open and she quickly pulls her hair loose from its ponytail so I know the interruption must be worth it.

"My name's Zac," the man says. His huge frame towers above us. Floppy blonde hair half covers his sparkling blue eyes. His toned and muscular legs are covered in sand and he grins down at us with a dazzling white smile.

"You must be our local champion," I say, my neck craned up at him, noticing his defined abs, not an inch to pinch anywhere.

He crouches down on his haunches and shakes both of our hands. "Finally I meet Billy's beautiful daughter," he says, gazing at me. "And who have we here? Her gorgeous friend, Daisy. There should be a law against having such stunning women grace our beaches. We're trying to surf here, and you two women are way too distracting."

We both titter like teenagers. The fact he knows our names is very flattering. He must have been talking to my dad. And who doesn't like a bit of male attention, especially when we are both nursing broken hearts and especially when it's coming from a god-like apparition with a deep tan.

"Perhaps we can hook up for a drink later?" Daisy suggests bravely.

"Nothing would please me more," he replies. "You two ladies have a good day now." He stands up. "I'll see you around. Excuse me, I need to catch a few waves while the going's good."

He strolls off and we both trail our eyes after him. His neat butt in long, black surfer shorts saunters along the shoreline and he picks up his surfboard, his rippling muscles moving as he lifts it up from the sand and carries it with him to the ocean.

"There you go, Daisy, the answer to your payback plot. Maybe you can give Johnny something to *genuinely* worry about."

"It's you he fancies," she tells me, an eyebrow raised.

"I don't think so. Didn't you see the way he eyed you up? Anyway, I'm too hung up on Alexandre." I sigh. "Still - can't complain about the attention."

Daisy lets out an exasperated groan. "And I'm too hung up on my bastard of a husband. Mind you, I wouldn't kick Zac out of bed on a cold rainy day."

We both burst into a cascade of giggles.

17

I t's raining in London. Gray, dull and depressing. No wonder
Alexandre prefers New York; even if it's cold in winter, the
skies are so often blue back home.

Daisy's mother is a sweetheart. She lives in a little house
in Hampstead near Hampstead Heath, a wild and sprawling park
where people take their dogs for rambling walks or play soccer on
Sundays. Although part of London, Hampstead is like a village
full of adorable pubs and quaint shops. Daisy's mum, Doris, has
set me up in a cozy room at the top of the house decorated with
flowery wallpaper – quintessentially English – and she's treating
me like a daughter – she misses Daisy so much.

I've done some wonderful sight-seeing here: the Crown
Jewels, Big Ben and the Houses of Parliament, Portobello Rd, a
street market on Friday and Saturday mornings where you can
pick up silver for nothing and vintage clothes. Actually, despite
the weather, this city really does have its charm. It feels like

dozens of villages melded together, each with their unique character. I've been going out with some of Daisy's friends who are more than welcoming. They have been taking me to local pubs, the theatre and walks along the Thames. The food in England is not the way it was when I came here as a teenager. Now, the cuisine is eclectic and plentiful with fabulous restaurants on every corner, the best of all being Indian food, inexpensive and delicious.

I have had some business meetings here, too. I couldn't justify to myself coming all this way to basically stalk Alexandre's ex-fiancée. I needed a better reason so I have visited some television stations – making a few connections and fanning about some ideas. The British have always done great documentaries – so far, I have been taken seriously and given a list of people to contact for future projects. Natalie needs my input more than ever.

I flew here straight from Hawaii with just a stop-over in LA. I couldn't face New York so I still haven't ventured into my new apartment and I haven't worked out what I'm going to do. I have called Alexandre several times but he is always too busy to discuss things in detail, or doesn't want to. He simply won't let me return the gifts. The Mercedes must be sitting in the garage in New York by now. I called Elodie. She had a wonderful trip with her friend driving across the States. It was she who provided me with Laura's address.

It is my final day here in London.

I have left the most daunting task until last.

I stand by Laura's front door nervously. It doesn't look dissimilar to number 10 Downing Street where the British Prime Minister lives, with a big brass knocker and letterbox. The wood is painted in a high gloss black, flanked by matching wrought-iron railings. It is all extremely 'grown-up' and intimidating. And it screams serious wealth. I wonder if Laura bought this place with all her modeling money or if her husband is rich. I seem to remember Alexandre once mentioning that he works in the City; a hedge-fund manager or something – the type that makes a million or two just for his Christmas bonus.

Finally, I pluck up the courage to rap the door knocker: the threatening head of a hefty brass lion.

Nobody answers.

My heart is pounding. Is it because I'm uninvited? Or that Alexandre was once so in love with Laura all those years ago? I don't know the answer but blood is drumming in my ears and my hands are clammy with trepidation. Finally, I hear footsteps.

The door opens slowly, guardedly. A head peeks out. By the way the person is dressed I guess that she's a member of staff. "May I help you?" the voice inquires with suspicion.

"Hi," I say beaming to try and hide my nerves. "I've come to see Laura."

"Mrs. Heimann?"

"Yes, is she in?"

"Do you have an invitation?"

Er, no. "I tried calling," I manage with a dry throat. *Why am I so nervous?*

"Who should I say is paying her a visit?"

Jeez, this is so formal. "Pearl."

"You're a pearl salesperson?"

"No, my name is Pearl. Pearl Robinson."

"Wait one moment please."

I am already feeling as small as a sparrow but when the door is closed on me, I feel as if I might as well be invisible. I wait. Five minutes later, the door opens. Wide. My jaw drops. A tall woman in her early thirties stands before me who is achingly beautiful. She must be at least five ten or eleven because I am like a shrinking violet in comparison. She's dressed in tight jeans, her legs go on forever. Her hair is wavy, long and blonde, her smile broad, with perfect, movie star teeth. She holds a black cane in her hand with a mother-of-pearl handle.

She greets me like a long-lost friend. "Pearl, come in."

I step into the immense hallway. The floors are white marble and a huge bunch of calla lilies adorns a big round table in the middle of the entrance, the table draped with pale blue shot-silk.

"Sorry, I wasn't expecting company, the place is a mess," she says with a faint giggle.

The 'place' is immaculate. Laura is immaculate.

I offer her my hand. "So nice to finally meet you. Alexandre always speaks…always *spoke*," I correct myself, "so fondly of you."

"Well, I'm sorry he's not here right now but he's been in a meeting all day – you know how it is with him? Always jetting off on a plane somewhere to make another deal, always wheeling and dealing. Come through, would you like some tea?"

Did I hear that right? 'Sorry, Alexandre isn't here right now?' No, she must have said his name by mistake. It must be her husband she's referring to.

I follow her through to a grand room. She has a slight limp but nothing you'd hardly notice. I look about me in awe. The walls are hung with what look like grand masters, the vast sash windows are letting in an afternoon glow. I notice she's wearing a huge ring on her engagement finger, not unlike mine.

She sits on a sofa and jingles a little bell. Her back is erect, her posture perfect. "I'll call for some tea and cake. I always get a bit peckish at this time of day," she says in a plummy British accent (like some aristocratic character out of the TV show, *Downton Abbey*).

"Did you mention Alexandre not being around?" I venture edgily.

The same woman who answered the door to me earlier comes in to the room. "You called, Madam?"

"Yes, Mrs. Blake. Tea for two please. Lapsang Souchong. Oh no, actually that might be a little too fancy for our American guest – make it basic PG Tips or whatever builders' tea we have." She smiles sweetly at me and I wonder if I have just heard correctly - *Too fancy for our American guest?? Builders' tea?*

"Where was I?" she continues in her posh accent. "Oh yes, Alexandre is out. He'll be so upset he missed you."

Alexandre? This is crazy, what does she mean? "Where's your husband?" I creak out, my mouth dry and parched. I need that tea even if it is only fit for builders.

"My soon to be ex-husband, you mean? Or are you referring to Alexandre, my fiancé?"

"You...and...Alexandre...are *seeing* each other again?" My brain is thumping with blood, I feel as if I'm about to collapse.

"Didn't he tell you?"

"I haven't spoken to him...I–"

"We're going to be married, Pearl."

"But...but...that's impossible! He was engaged to me, he was

244

going to marry *me*. You're not divorced yet, Alexandre would never—"

"Well, we're an item again. He had a little…what should we call it…a detour. With you. You were the rebound, Pearl, his solace after a broken heart. I'm sorry, it must be very painful to hear this but…well…he's always been in love with me, surely you guessed that?"

My hands are shaking, my breathing pinched. I think of all those books of hers still at his house in Provence. "But you were happily married to—"

"We never stopped loving each other, Alexandre and I."

"You're *sleeping* with him?" I cry out, trying to keep control of my frayed nerves.

She cackles with laughter. "*Sleeping* is not exactly the word I'd use."

"But he was…he was in love with *me*."

"No, Pearl. He was in 'lust' with you, for a brief spell. But he never had me out of his thoughts, not for a second. You were – oh, I'm sorry, would you like a tissue, there, there, don't cry now."

But I can't help it. Tears are flowing down my cheeks. She hands me a box of Kleenex and I snivel and blow my running nose into a wad of them, but there aren't enough to soak up my gushing tears. I'm making a complete spectacle of myself and am about to get up and leave but her cell phone rings. My curiosity is peeked. She answers and starts speaking perfect, fluent French; laughing and joking. I feel sick. Her French is perfect, *she's* perfect. Stunning. Intelligent. And the worst thing of all? Alexandre has been in love with her the whole time. She ends her call and beams at me.

"That was Sophie, she's coming over in an hour. Do stay, I'm sure she'd love to see you."

"But you said Sophie was dangerous. That she tried to kill you!"

"No, surely not?"

My voice hitches and heaves, "You called me, Laura, and told me not to go to Vegas, that Sophie could 'top me off,' that she had politicians and police in her pocket and…and…"

"Oh, poor Pearl, so gullible. I just didn't want Alexandre to marry you. I had to stop him somehow."

"So it was all a lie about Sophie?"

She lays her cane down and smoothes her slim hand over her luscious blonde locks. "Sophie's a pussycat at heart. Okay, she can be a bit frosty sometimes but it's just her manner. In fact, if she says mean things it's her way of communicating. It's when she's silent you have to watch out. I can't believe you thought she was out to kill you." She laughs raucously. "Alexandre told me as much - that you were suffering from delusions about Sophie. Tut-tut, Pearl, not the best way to warm him up, you know how close they are. You couldn't have picked a better way to alienate yourself from him. Oh, and bossing him around the way you did. Not the best of moves."

I can't believe what I'm hearing. Sweet, charity-giving Laura is a total bitch!

She widens her huge, blue eyes and talks on. "Ironically, Sophie actually rather likes you, likes your quirkiness. It took me *years* for her to warm up to me, yet you…well, you two could have been friends if you'd given her more of a chance. She's had a shit life so she's a bit tough on the outside but actually, she's really sweet when you get to know her."

I am silent now. The sound of my tears has been taken over by my heartbeat which feels as if it's about to explode in my chest.

"So how did your accident happen? Nothing to do with Sophie, then?" I ask.

"Of course not! It was bad luck, that's all. A load of children's toys had been left on the steps. I was tipsy. I tripped. I fell. End of story."

"But it's not the end of the story! You split Alexandre and me up! You told me a lie!" I screech at her.

"Far better that you broke up before that silly marriage of yours took place. Alexandre would have come back to me no matter what, even if it meant divorce. He's been desperately in love with me Pearl, from the day we met. And I with him."

"Then why did you marry your husband...James?"

"Because I was a cripple, for fuck's sake. You think I wanted Alexandre to look after me, to shackle him like a slave to a disabled person? I loved him too much for that. Besides, he had no money then. He was just starting up his company, he didn't have a bean – I needed stability, someone who could look after me properly."

"You *used* your husband?"

"James wanted to be with me. It wasn't 'using' him. But the moment I was really better, able to lead a normal life...well, it seemed right that Alexandre and I should get back together. I mean literally, all I had to do was click my fingers and he was waiting for me. He'd been hoping all along, that's why he's always been in touch and remained friends just in case, in case I changed my mind. All this physical slog I've put my body through - the physiotherapy I've been slaving away at - has been so we can be a normal, functional couple again."

She used her husband as a means to an end. I want to shout at her but all I can do is start blubbering again like a child who has fallen off a bicycle she realizes is too big for her to manage.

"Now, now Pearl, don't cry. You've come away with all sorts of goodies – he's been more than generous when he didn't need to be. Two fuck-off apartments, two fuck-off cars, a ready-made business, all sorts of gorgeous jewelry, oh, and let's not forget that Birkin bag I see you carrying. Obviously you could never afford to buy that for yourself. Alexandre offered me a Birkin but I thought it was too passé – preferred a Kelly, myself. But still, do you have any idea how much that's worth? That color is unusual – looks like a one-off. That handbag must have cost a bloody fortune, not to mention the fact that there's a queue as long as my arm to even get one in the first place. Alexandre must have pulled some serious strings. That pretty bag probably cost him…ooh, I don't know, upwards of forty grand. Fitting, really, that it should cost forty grand when you're forty. Beyond generous, I'd say. So why, Pearl, are you feeling so sorry for yourself?"

The way she uses 'fuck-off' as an adjective to describe something fabulous is typically British – I've heard it before - yet it rings in my ears as if I have been punched in the head. 'Fuck off' – that is basically what Alexandre has done – told me to fuck off, yet sweetened it with all his amazing gifts. But nothing has been sweet, just sour and bitter. And this is the sourest news of all.

I manage to get out in a rasp, "I don't *care* about material stuff, it's Alexandre I want."

Laura tosses her head. "Well, you're too late. And anyway, he was fond of you, it's true, but he thinks you're a total loony. All that lesbian bondage nonsense - oh and your slutty past. So not his style."

No! he would never share that – it's my personal life! "He told you?" I ask incredulously.

"Of course he did, we don't hold any secrets from each other."

"But that's not like him, he would never do that."

"I'm his best friend, Pearl, as well as his true love – he tells me everything, he confides in me. He can't believe he took you so seriously. Look, I have to be cruel to be kind here…" she lowers her voice almost to a whisper… "he *doesn't* love you. He never really has. You had a laugh, that's all. You had some steamy sex, maybe, but it's *me* he loves. And besides, you couldn't even give him a child. He wants a family. You and he were all wrong right from the word go. Do yourself a favor, Pearl, get over him, find yourself a nice American boy with whom you have something in common."

"Alexandre and I had so much in common!"

"Bollocks. You Americans don't get our acerbic sense of humor. You're all so earnest and, 'have a nice day'. We're different from you lot. You need someone more your own age, too. Ah, look the tea's arrived. Do you take milk?"

Mrs. Blake waddles in with a tray. I get up, unsteady on my feet. I feel as if I'm going to faint. "No thank you, I need to go."

"Please yourself. I'll tell Alexandre you dropped by."

I turn around. I need to know one last thing. "What about Rex?"

She throws up her hands. "Rex? Well, we'll have him shipped over here, of course. I hate New York, wouldn't dream of living in that shithole so we'll be in London full time. That's when we're not wintering in the Caribbean, that is. I'm not big on dogs but you know, he's Alex's pride and joy so I suppose I'll have to deal with the creature."

The *creature? Alex?* I want to slap her face and would but she'd probably beat me with her witch's cane.

I slowly begin to slink out of the house feeling like the most worthless human being alive.

Laura remains cheery and nauseatingly jolly, waving as I leave. But just as I reach the door she calls after me, "Shame about your divine Zang Toi wedding dress - what a waste."

I pretend I don't hear. It's as if she has sucked out all my energy with her painful words. I have no gumption, no force or ammunition left inside me to defend myself. There I was talking with Daisy about women needing armor and I had none. I feel shamed. My head is slung low like a beaten dog, I pad out of the house, my misery trailing me like a murky shadow.

I am so crushed and weak that I decide to sit on a park bench by the square that faces her grand house to regroup my fragmented dignity. I get out my iPod and put on the first song I see – the Blues - Billie Holiday, *Foolin' Myself.* How apt. I stay there for a good few minutes mulling over all the cruel but probably truthful things Laura has told me, or rather, fired at me like a relentless machine gun. I agree with Billie Holiday, I *am* through with love and I'll have nothing more to do with love. What's the point ever opening myself up again? Even if I had gone through with the marriage in Vegas with Alexandre, it would have, at some point, come to an abrupt end. Alexandre is still in love with Laura. As she said, I was just a 'detour'. The 'rebound'.

I think of my beautiful wedding gown probably being worked on right now. Crystals being hand-sewn on the train, the exquisite silk smoothed and pressed, a myriad of tiny, feminine fingers working on all the details. I noticed Zang Toi had mostly women in his atelier, busy as dedicated bees, their keen eyes supervising every fine stitch, every delicate fold. What am I going to do about that dress, that work of art? The truth is it would be better off in a museum.

And just when I'm praying that there may have been some mistake, some misunderstanding, or that it could all be a fantasy on Laura's part, Reality slaps me in the face. I see the thing I'm dreading most in the world - Alexandre approach Laura's front door.

I observe the scene, wishing I could look away but I am transfixed. He's holding what looks like a gift-wrapped box. She opens the door, tosses her golden mane and throws her loving arms around his broad shoulders.

Then the glossy black door with its brass lion's head shuts with a bang and I feel as if it has slammed right in my face.

It wasn't Sophie who was my enemy. No.

It's been Laura all along.

I 'm still staring in disbelief at Laura's sinister, black, front door. I have not moved from this park bench. The only thing that has changed in the last ten minutes is the music I'm listening to on my iPod. The Blues have been replaced with Patsy Cline's *Sweet Dreams*. That is all I have left – dreams of Alexandre and memories of how it used to be between us. Could I really have just imagined the intensity of our bond, our passion? 'He was in lust with you,' Laura told me, just twenty minutes ago, and I now see that what she said was true. Alexandre walked through her door. What more proof do I need that it is over between us?

He is still in love with her, his ex fiancée. This horrific fact is seeping through my veins like green poison, sapping me of energy, rendering me drained, making me feel as if my life has been nothing but a lie for the last five months.

Laura's words, 'rebound' and 'detour' to describe who and what I am to Alexandre are ringing in my ears. Twice, I have tried to get up from where I'm sitting. I want to rap at that foreboding, black door and confront him, but my muscles are weak – I can hardly move. Laura has been plotting and scheming to get him back all along and he was waiting, as she said, for her to click her fingers.

Click.

And he rushed back to her like an eager dog.

I fumble about in my beautiful, red Birkin bag for my cell phone. I need to speak to Alessandra Demarr. Maybe she can clear a few things up for me.

My memory slides back to that moment when I fled Alessandra's house, when I found that photo of her and Sophie together in an intimate embrace. I had the notion that they had set me up and that Sophie was trying to destroy my life by wheedling herself in on my film projects; infiltrating her way into HookedUp Enterprises. Alexandre testified to her innocence, swore that her motivation came from nothing more than her desire to help out her girlfriend and get us out of a sticky situation when Samuel Myers wasn't good for the money. I didn't believe him. But now I see that Alexandre could have been telling the truth. I have been so 'hooked up' on Sophie that I was blind to what was really going on… Laura, my real enemy from word, Go.

Laura told me that Sophie actually liked me, confirming what Alexandre had also said. Either I am living some sort of Hitchcockian nightmare, where everyone is conspiring to drive me to a loony bin, or they're right – I have misjudged Sophie – wrongly accused her. There I was, obsessing about my future sister-in-law, when it was Laura I should have been looking out for, all along.

Alessandra picks up her phone after several rings. She sounds groggy and I realize that it's only eight a.m. Los Angeles time; she isn't an early riser. Too bad, I can't wait. Rise. And. Shine.

"It's Pearl," I say with urgency. "Sorry to wake you."

I hear a growling yawn. "Can you call back, I was sleeping - I thought it was a family emergency." Her sleepiness is evident - her Italian accent is more pronounced than usual.

"Well, considering that you and I could have been family, it is."

"What are you talking about, Pearl?"

253

"Alessandra, I'm so sorry to wake you and everything, but I'm not in a good way and I really need to talk."

"If this is about *Stone Trooper—*"

"It's about Sophie, your girlfriend, my ex-to-be sister-in-law." I am aware of how crazy that sounds. I do up the top button of my coat – the London humidity is getting into my bones. My eyes are still fixed on Laura's front door as I hold my cell next to my ear in my other shaky hand. I need answers and I need them now.

Alessandra's voice suddenly perks up with interest. "Did Sophie tell you that she and I were a couple?"

"I found a photo of you two in your kitchen, and Alexandre confirmed to me that Sophie was gay."

"Don't you *dare* say anything to Sophie about us, Pearl - about that night. *Please!*" She is pleading; the desperation and fear in her voice takes me by surprise.

"So you and Sophie weren't playing some game on me? Some, 'let's screw with Pearl's head' kind of game?"

She chuckles – her laugh is laced with irony. "What? Are you *insane?*"

"It just seemed all too much of a coincidence; that I was working on *Stone Trooper*…suddenly Sophie gets involved… you coming on board at the perfect moment and then seducing me…"

"Look, can we talk about this later? I need a coffee. I can't even think straight right now."

"Alessandra. I'm sitting outside Laura's house in London and she just so happens to be - not only Alexandre's ex-freaking-fiancée - but his *present* fiancée as well. He's inside her house, as we speak. He's involved with her again. No, let me spell that out – *he is going to marry her*, she is divorcing her husband. She's all

254

buddy-buddy with Sophie and−"

"What? Sophie hates that money-grabbing bitch!"

Did I just hear that right? "But Alexandre said they were friends."

"Sophie puts up with her," Alessandra informs me in her husky voice, all the more husky for being the morning. "She's never liked Laura. Anyway, I don't think she's seen or spoken to her for ages."

I squeal out, "But I was at Laura's house, just now, and she said Sophie was coming over! They spoke on the phone. In French, no less."

"I doubt that, Pearl. Look, I'm sleepy, can we speak later?"

"Wait! No. Alessandra...why, when we were in LA were you referring to Sophie as your 'ex' if you're still together?"

"Questions, questions."

"Please Alessandra!"

"We had a big fight − she said I was using her to get ahead in my career. All because, I was too busy to speak to her one time. That was just before you arrived in LA She told me it was over. So I had some fun with you to spite her."

"You were planning on telling Sophie about us to make her jealous?"

"No, of course not. I'm not that dumb. She'd come after us both with a carving knife. But it made me smile inside − you know, knowing I had the last laugh. Sorry, Pearl, I have to admit...I was using you to make myself feel better. Can I hang up now?"

"No! I need to know more about Laura."

"I've never met her," Alessandra replies boredly, punctuated by a yawn.

My heart sinks. I remember Laura's words: *'He was fond of you, it's true, but he thinks you're a total loony. All that lesbian bondage nonsense - oh and your slutty past...'*

I had assumed Sophie had enlightened Laura, but from what Alessandra says, obviously not. The only other person that knew about my adventure with Alessandra Demarr was Alexandre, himself. *How did Laura know those intimate details of my sex life?* Simple – he must have told her. She was speaking the truth. He confides in her, even when it comes to me. I feel so belittled.

Belittled. And cheap.

Alessandra pipes up, "Anyway, Pearl, as I was saying, Sophie is not a big fan of Laura's. Apparently, Laura has been sniffing about Alexandre again showing real interest. Her husband has lost a lot of capital in the stock market, or is being done for some dodgy dealings tax-wise and no longer has the kind of money he had before. So Sophie thinks she's after Alexandre because of what he can offer her."

"What does Sophie say about *me*?" I ask, wondering if Sophie is suspicious of everyone who comes near her brother.

"You really want to know?"

My heart starts pounding – might as well hear the worst. "Yes."

"She thinks you're the best thing to happen to Alexandre for years. At first, she suspected that you were like all the other women after him – interested primarily in money. But when you told him you wanted to do a pre-nup and refused to take a stake in HookedUp Enterprises, she knew you loved him for *him*."

Wouldn't everyone love him for him? "Why is she still so bitchy, then?"

"It's part of her DNA, Pearl. But if you made more of an

effort, you'd find she'd be a good friend to you. She said that, too. That you didn't like her, that you still hadn't forgiven her, and that you were a hard nut to crack."

"She said all this in English? Hard nut to crack?"

"Of course not. You know how bad her English is – we speak in French."

"You speak French? I didn't know that."

"Well, Pearl – there's a lot you don't know about me. Just keep quiet about our little evening, will you?"

"Are you kidding me? Of course. Anyway, I don't have anyone to tell even if I wanted to. It's over between Alexandre and me."

"Nonsense. Latin passion can escalate or descend at any moment – he'll be back."

"That's just it, Alessandra. He broke up with me in a cold, passionless voice. And now he's seeing Laura again. Not just seeing her but sleeping with her. She's like some top model...I don't stand a chance."

"You say you're outside Laura's house and Alexandre is inside? Go and knock at the door, silly. I'm going back to sleep, Pearl. Remember, don't you *dare* tell Sophie about what happened or you'll regret it."

"Is that a Sicilian threat?"

"You bet."

Revenge is a dish best served cold. "Don't worry, Alessandra, my lips are sealed. You think I want Sophie running after me with a carving knife? Thanks for talking to me - things are a lot clearer now. Good night, morning - whatever. Sleep well."

The line clicks dead.

I take a deep breath and stand up. I have a head-rush – black stars flicker behind my eyes. Laura's front door is giving me heart palpitations. Black as the Devil himself, it beckons me and taunts me mockingly. *Come, come and humiliate yourself.*

But Alessandra's right. I need to see Alexandre face to face.

I stand at the door, once again. It is so glossy I see my warped reflection before me. A disheveled woman who is forty whole years old. No wonder Alexandre has gone back to glamorous Laura. I rap the lion's brass knocker head. The lion is saying to me, *I challenge you, go on – make a fool out of yourself, see if I care.*

I knock three times. Rap, rap, rap. My heart…pound, pound, pound.

Nothing.

I'm planning in my head everything I'm going to say: *Alexandre, please be honest with me, please…*

The smooth black door swings open. Not Mrs. Blake but Laura, herself.

I will not cry, I will not cry. Be strong, no tears, no scene…be strong.

She's standing there, looking like some figurehead on a ship; tall, willowy, in a royal blue, silk-satin dressing gown shimmering about her slim body like ripples of water. My heart sinks. She has that just-fucked look – the afternoon love-making flush glowing in her cheeks. Her hair is all mussed up. She says coyly, "Pearl, what a surprise!" Her smile is set like a plastic bride on a wedding cake. "What can I do for you?"

"I need to speak to Alexandre," I reply bravely.

"Sorry, but he's not here. He just left."

My composure melts into the damp sidewalk. "Don't lie to me, Laura. I saw him come in through this door twenty minutes ago. He's here!"

"My word, have you been spying on us?" Her smirk is victorious.

I try to stick my foot in the door. "Let me in. I need to see him, just for a few minutes and then I'll be on my way."

"Pearl, I'm not making this up. He left five minutes ago."

"BULLSHIT! I've been watching your front door. Nobody has left, least of all Alexandre."

"You don't know much about London houses, do you? This house's garden backs onto our mews house and garages. He went out the back."

"Laura, you've gotten what you wanted. Why are you tormenting me? Please, I just want to see him for—"

"God, you're a bore. Do I have to spell it out? HE. IS. NOT. HERE! Go round the back and see for yourself if you don't believe me."

"What was he doing here?" I demand, my body shaking with rage.

"Now you're being naïve. He just fucked me senseless, if you must know. You're not the only one who likes a little afternoon sex, Pearl. Now run along, I have stuff to do." She begins to push the door in my face.

And then I shout out something cruel. Something I know I'll regret. Words spill uncontrollably from my mouth:

"I wish you'd stayed in your freaking wheel chair forever!"

The lid is firmly in the coffin now. Not only am I jilted, I am despicable. When Alexandre hears what I have just said, he'll be shocked and never want anything to do with me again.

It's official.

I'm a jealous, spiteful, malicious bitch.

Laura slams the door in my face.

I scamper around the block to see if what Laura said about a mews house and garage is true. It is. Only the extremely wealthy could afford to have their garden sandwiched between two stunning houses in one of the most expensive areas in London. The mews is cobbled – in the olden days this is where the stables for horses and carriages were but now, of course, just a mews house alone in this Chelsea neighborhood would set you back millions, let alone adjoining garages. I imagine Laura's husband, James, beavering away in the City to buy all this for the woman he's in love with, for whom he sacrificed his life – and now she is about to dump him because he's no longer rich enough for her. Does Alexandre know who he is dealing with? That Laura is as ruthless as a razor blade? Like most men who are smitten, he probably doesn't see through her sweetness and light act.

A thought suddenly rushes to my brain. Uh, oh. I just insulted her, said the worst possible thing somebody can say and she'll be out for revenge. Laura knows about me and Alessandra. All it takes is one phone call to Sophie.

The carving knife…

I call Alessandra again.

She sighs into the phone, exasperated. "What d'you want now, Pearl?"

"Laura knows about us. About…our evening," I stutter. "Just warning you."

"Deny, deny, deny. And I suggest you do the same. How the fuck would Laura *know* that?"

"Alexandre must have told her."

"Thanks, Pearl, for sharing that with him - now I'll have *him* after me with a carving knife, too."

"No, you won't – he really didn't…doesn't care. I'm history."

"I didn't know he was the tattle-tale-tit type."

"He's not. He's usually very discreet; it's not like him at all."

"Well thanks for the warning," she says grumpily. "Bye."

I amble back to Sloane Street and walk towards Knightsbridge. I have a couple of hours to kill before I need to go back to Hampstead for my suitcase and make my way to Heathrow for my flight. I get my iPod out of my bag and go through the playlist. Got it. The perfect 'fuck you' song ever written, Gloria Gaynor's *I Will Survive*. The music feels great. Powerful. Encouraging. Hell, I even feel like disco dancing along the street. I punch my arm in the air. Yes, I *am* strong and I *will* survive. I refuse to mooch about and feel sorry for myself. Life goes on and we women can be tough. I *am* tough. I'm a New Yorker for crying out loud! I can do it. I will survive, I sing out loud and I don't care who hears me, even if I'm out of tune.

Where to head now? Harrods, why not? Probably the most famous department store in the world. I'll go there and buy a gift for Daisy's mother to say thank you for my stay. Perhaps some home-made chocolates or some fancy bath salts.

I step through revolving doors, greeted by uniformed doormen and make my way through the vast labyrinth of the store to the Food Hall. There is no place like it; I could be stepping into a museum. My mother brought me to this emporium and I vowed I'd return one day. It's a work of art. This was the original part of the shop, opened in the first half of the nineteenth century. Now Harrods is comprised of seven floors and spans an incredible four and a half acres. I have never seen such opulence and grandeur where food is sold. It is like a food court at a palace – something worthy of Louis IV or some bygone monarch's banquet feast.

The black and white marble floors stretch before me like a long yawn and the imposing molding decorating the ceiling reminds you that this building is a majestic legend – a true London landmark. Hall after hall is grandly overflowing with beautifully presented gourmet food delights. My eyes and nose are already feasting. The sheer volume and selection of British and International goods is awe inspiring - artisan chocolates, lavish cuts of meat and seafood - even exotic things like sea urchin. Unusual cheeses, Dim Sum, Beluga caviar, truffle butter, pistachio and rose Turkish delights, gourmet terrines and drool-worthy patisserie - all presented in breathtakingly beautiful displays arranged behind gleaming glass counters. It is like being in the hall of mirrors in Versailles, only with food, reflected twenty-fold by mirrors set in arches, made glorious by mahogany and brass light fixtures – everything twinkling and glittering in gold.

Foolishly, I thought I could whip in and out of here, but I am mesmerized by the beauty of the place, the surreal Willy Wonka and the Chocolate Factory I-want-it-all attack. Where to begin? What to buy? You could spend a week in the Food Halls alone, not to mention the rest of Harrods. I get some exquisite French truffles for Daisy's mum, Doris, and meander towards another tempting counter.

I'm staring at cupcakes now. I need some kind of American comfort food after the Laura 'encounter.' What to choose? – Banana, Mocha, Strawberry, Rocky Road, Sticky Toffee…or the chocolate torte sprinkled with gold dust? Edible art if ever I saw it.

"Pearl, is zat you?" a voice exclaims behind my shoulders.

I nearly jump out of my skin. I see a familiar reflection in the mirror before me.

It is Sophie.

I spin around in amazement, my sneakers squeaking on the polished marble floor. A nervous guilty churn makes my stomach dip. Sophie with her carving knife…does she know about me and Alessandra?

Obviously not, because she is smiling, and for the first time her happiness seems to be genuine. Or is that just me? Now that I know she doesn't hate my guts, I can observe her with fresh eyes, devoid of judgment and suspicion.

"What are you doing in London?" she asks, kissing me on both cheeks. I inhale her usual, heady scent of *Fracas* and notice how pretty she's looking, her eyes are like pools of dark chocolate and she's dressed immaculately in a chic, navy blue pantsuit. Hand-tailored, no doubt. I know she and Alexandre get all their suits cut on Savile Row, here in London.

"I came…I…I had some work appointments," I splutter.

"What a wonderfool surprise. Alexandre never told me you were both here."

Wonder Fool. Fool being the operative word. *So you don't know we broke up? That he dumped me? That he's gone back to Laura?* "I'm leaving today," I say simply. "Back to New York."

"What a shame, we could have hooked up. Isn't zis place marvelloose? I come here to get my Jelly Belly jelly beans. Cannot get zem anywhere, you know. My little American addiction." She holds up the bag of candy. Jelly Belly – my favorites, too.

I want to spill it all out and tell Sophie my woes. I want to discuss everything and ask her about Laura; tell her that Laura warned me that she would 'top me off' in order to stop me marrying Alexandre in Vegas - but I am dumbstruck, not least by the bizarre coincidence of bumping into Sophie here at Harrods – what are the odds of that?

"Where do you go now? You want a coffee? Or razzer, in England a cup of tea, no?

"I have a plane to catch, I need to get back to Hampstead, then get my case and catch the tube to Heathrow," I reply uneasily.

"Hampstead? Alexandre usually stays at zee Connaught."

Sophie doesn't know?? "I'm visiting a friend," I say uneasily. "Alexandre isn't with me."

"My driver, he can take you to Hampstead and zen airport, okay? Save so much time. I have a friend in Hampstead I've been wanting to see forever. We go togezzer." She links her arm with mine and ushers me through the crowds, and out of Harrods. Her embrace is warm and I wonder…was it me? Was I the one, all along, who has been spiky and defensive? Maybe Alexandre was right. Sophie has been trying to be my friend for months.

I caused all that trouble for nothing. I wish, now, I could jump into a time capsule and travel back to the waiting private jet at Van Nuys Airport.

But it's all too late.

Shadows of Pearl Playlist

Lullaby - Brahms

Autumn in New York - Sarah Vaughn

Hotel California - The Eagles

Surfin' USA - The Beach Boys

Woman - Neneh Cherry

Witchcraft - Frank Sinatra

I Kissed a Girl and I Liked It - Katy Perry

Leaving on a Jet Plane - John Denver (Sung by Chantal Kreviazuk)

She's a Rainbow - The Rolling Stones

Foolin' Myself - Billie Holiday

To listen to the Shadows of Pearl soundtrack:
http://ariannerichmonde.com/music/shadows-of-pearl-of-pearl-sound-track/

Thank you so much for reading my book which I hope you enjoyed. For more information about me please visit my website: www.ariannerichmonde.com

Available at Amazon

Part 1 of *The Pearl Trilogy*, **Shades of Pearl**
Part 3 of *The Pearl Trilogy*, **Shimmers of Pearl**
You can also get the entire collection of
The Pearl Trilogy

I have also written ***Glass, a short story.***

Join me on Facebook:
http://facebook.com/AuthorArianneRichmonde

Twitter: @A_Richmonde

If you would like to be the first to know about my next book release please go to: http://ariannerichmonde.com/email-signup/
Your details are private and will not be shared with anyone else. You can unsubscribe at any time.

I love hearing from readers. Feel free to send me an email at ariannerichmonde@gmail.com.

Made in the USA
San Bernardino, CA
25 October 2013